I0213520

THE RHYTHM
OF THE GAME

JEFF CURTIS

Copyright © 2012
The Rhythm of the Game Jeff Curtis

All rights reserved.
All rights reserved. Except as permitted under the US Copyright Act
of 1976, the contents of this book may not be reproduced,
transmitted, or distributed in any part or by any means without the
prior written consent of the author and/or publisher.

Published by Distractions Ink
P.O. Box 15971
Rio Rancho, NM 87174

©Copyright 2012 by Jeff Curtis
Cover Photography by ©Tom Smart/Deseret News
and ©Brian Jackson/Dreamstime.com
Additional photography courtesy Tom Smart/Deseret News
Cover Design and Interior Graphics by
Sandy Ann Allred/Timeless Allure

First Printed Edition: October 2012

Curtis, Jeff, 1962—
The Rhythm of the Game: a novel/by Jeff Curtis.

ISBN: 978-0-9884276-6-2

Library of Congress Control Number: 2012952423

Printed in the United States of America

Acknowledgments

"I long to possess beauty, to acquire it, collect it, to hold it in my hands." – Delose Conner, *Very Basic Art Lessons*

I love beautiful things. I yearn to see beauty; I yearn to hear beauty; I yearn to hold beauty. I have attempted to capture beauty here. Thanks for your help, Delose. If indeed I have captured something beautiful, it wouldn't have happened without you.

I love to dream. Lafe Conner inspired me with this quote about dreams:

"The future belongs to those who believe in the beauty of their dreams." – Eleanor Roosevelt.

Thank you, Lafe, for adding clarity to the beauty of my dreams.

I love my wife. Thank you, Kristi, for creating. Thank you for allowing me to see, to hear, and to hold the beautiful Amanda, Tyler, Blake, and Aubree.

I love anyone who loves my children. Thank you, Marcia and Kevin, for loving Amanda, Tyler, Blake, and Aubree. And thanks for asking. I didn't have the courage to come to you; yet you were willing to come to me and ask. This whole thing would be just another Word document on my hard drive if it weren't for you.

I love Amanda, Tyler, Blake, and Aubree. This book is for Blake. Thank you, Blake, for just being you. Those who read will see truth if, in spite of my weakness, your beauty has been captured within these pages.

To the Petersens.
When we finished the season, you told me I should write a book.
I took you up on it. I hope it's what you thought it would be.

Contents

Chapter One—Epiphany

"Are you ready for your first solo delivery?" Sharon asked.

Sharon was my new boss. She managed the local pizza joint. I felt too old to be delivering pizzas, but times were difficult. I still had decent work, but the decreased commission from the downturn had left me no alternative but to find a second job. The August evening in Kaysville was sultry. My new delivery uniform was completely black, and I rationalized that the combination of the color, the heat, and the stillness of the evening made me feel uncomfortable. I was only kidding myself. I felt uncomfortable because I was delivering pizza to support my family. Pride swallowed, I stood up straight, all in black, and forced a reply. "Yes," was all I could muster. I gathered the two bags of hot pizza and walked toward the door. *The only good thing about this uniform is I get to wear a ball cap to cover my bald head*, I mused as I continued toward the jeep. Sharon stopped me before I could escape.

"Remember to tuck in your shirt."

I paused, swallowed my pride again, and followed her instruction. I was already the delivery boy; tucking in my shirt couldn't add to the insult.

The delivery took me south to Farmington. As I crossed the city line, my mind drifted. I thought of the baseball diamond tucked away behind the elementary school. That diamond had been the source of many happy memories for my sons and me. The daydream ended abruptly as I approached the house for the delivery. It was a beautiful home, made completely of brick. There were two vehicles in the open garage that were both much nicer than my son's rusted old jeep. Every blade of grass in the well-manicured lawn was perfect. I felt envy as I climbed the front steps.

"I'm glad at least someone has been able to hang on."

I focused on the delivery as the owner of the home appeared and walked toward me. About my same age, he smiled as he approached. As he neared, he paused. The moment was awkward. I felt as though I were back in school. I felt as if I had just been escorted to the principal's office. I recognized his face, but I couldn't place him. When I took the delivery job, I was certain to chance upon someone I knew who was not caught up in a similar struggle. I had hoped, however, the meeting would not be so early in my "career." I needed time to prepare. But the confrontation was here, now, on my first solo run. I decided to make the best of it.

"Here's the pizza you ordered!" I blurted out as I forced a smile and pushed the pizza bags toward him. I thought I commanded my emotions well as I waited for his answer. There was another pause, more awkward than the first. Then he spoke.

"Didn't you coach in the Farmington baseball league?"

I still couldn't place the man, but there was no point in lying.

"Yes. I still do," I said with another smile. "You probably remember me more for Blake than anything else. We've played baseball in the Farmington league for years."

I didn't have to force a smile as I spoke of Blake. Thoughts of Blake would carry me through the ordeal. He was one of five reasons—my wife and the rest of my children were the other four—that I had taken the second job. Thoughts of the beauty nearest me always make me smile.

"Blake is the only boy with Down syndrome ever to play in the Farmington league."

"What division did you play in this season?"

"We were in the Bronco Division. We did quite well this year." My body temperature seemed to increase exponentially under the black uniform as I stood in the evening sun. It was time to move the conversation forward. "I have a son in college right now, and I'm just trying to make ends meet. That's why I'm delivering pizzas."

"What's the total?" he asked.

"It's $41.60."

"Just a minute. I didn't know how much pizza the girls ordered. I'll be right back."

I stood alone on the porch as the man disappeared into his home. It seemed forever before he returned. He reappeared and put the cash for the pizza in my hand. It was important to make sure there was enough money to cover the delivery, but I was in no mood to prolong the process. I didn't glance at the bills I was holding.

"Can I get you some change?"

"No, keep it. We'll watch for you next season."

I hurried back to the jeep. I wanted to run, and not just run to the jeep. I wanted to run as far away as I could, but again I tried to control my emotions. The homeowner disappeared inside. It was dark. As I sat in the jeep, I took a moment to collect my thoughts and confirm there was enough money for the delivery. It wouldn't be wise to return to the pizzeria short of cash. There was still time to make up the difference if the amount were off. I counted twenty extra dollars and started to cry. I considered taking the money back to the generous giver, but for the third time that evening, I swallowed hard. I started the jeep's engine and drove away. The man's intentions were nothing but honorable, but those intentions didn't make it any easier to accept the gift.

In *The Legend of Bagger Vance*, the caddie-slash-philosopher Bagger gave insight to Rannulph Junuh:

> Inside each and every one of us is one true authentic swing. Something we was born with. Something that's ours and ours alone. Something that can't be taught to you or learned, something that got to be remembered. Over time the world can rob us of that swing. It get buried inside us and all our wouldas and couldas and shouldas. Some folk even forget what their swing was like.[1]

Perhaps difficulty causes us to search for the swing that has been robbed from us. Tears flowed freely down my face as I drove back to the pizzeria. How could I keep delivering if I had to face this every night? I was deeply grateful, but it wasn't gifts I wanted. I wanted to take care of my family. I tried to regain control. I worried Sharon would wonder what she'd done if she saw the old bald guy she hired crying when he returned from his first delivery.

Did the universe have a beginning? If the universe is eternal, if there was no beginning and there is no end, can remembering forgotten truth restore our own eternity? Memories of my authentic swing began to return. Collecting my thoughts, I repeated the only exercise I knew to recover from such difficult emotion. I thought of my five reasons, and I thought of Blake. Blake made it easy to smile through tears. Thoughts of Blake as he played in the Farmington Area Baseball League (FABL) filled my memory. The sounds, the smells, and the sights of Blake playing

---

1   "One True Authentic Swing," *The Legend of Bagger Vance*, directed by Robert Redford (Universal City, CA: Dreamworks Pictures and Twentieth Century Fox, 2000), DVD.

on the Bronco Field could make anyone smile. The crunch of Blake's spikes digging into the dirt on the first base path was music for all to hear; the perfume of the freshly dampened infield where Blake stood was a delight for all to inhale; the light in Blake's eyes as he took his turn at bat was a vision for all to see. Blake William Curtis is the only player with Down syndrome to ever play in the FABL. He is a mockingbird.

A mockingbird?

In *To Kill a Mockingbird,* Harper Lee defined mockingbirds. She described the grace, the sacredness, and the beauty of the birds through Scout. Scout explained how she came to know mockingbirds through her father, Atticus.

> When he gave us our air-rifles Atticus wouldn't teach us to shoot. Uncle Jack instructed us in the rudiments thereof; he said Atticus wasn't interested in guns. Atticus said to Jem one day, "I'd rather you shot at tin cans in the back yard, but I know you'll go after birds. Shoot all the blue jays you want, if you can hit 'em, but remember it's a sin to kill a mockingbird."
>
> That was the only time I ever heard Atticus say it was a sin to do something, and I asked Miss Maudie about it.
>
> "Your father's right," she said. "Mockingbirds don't do one thing but make music for us to enjoy. They don't eat up people's gardens, don't nest in corncribs, they don't do one thing but sing their hearts out for us. That's why it's a sin to kill a mockingbird."[2]

In the world of pizza deliveries, time is not a fixed construct. As I gathered myself to return to the pizzeria, memories of a lifetime of baseball with Blake poured through my consciousness. I thought

---

2   Harper Lee, *To Kill a Mockingbird* (New York: Harper Collins, 1995), 103.

of the night, a magical night, when the Farmington Bronco Field became the center of a universe, the Home Base for mockingbirds.

Worlds and universes took notice when Blake played baseball on that magical night. Although a boy with Down syndrome, Blake was handsome, fourteen years old, with a boys-of-summer tan, blonde hair, blue eyes, and a devilishly captivating smile. Note that I did not write Blake was "a Down syndrome boy." The boy comes before the Down syndrome.

Blake's smile's captivation wasn't found in the corners of his mouth, though they did turn up slowly, gently, and with a hint of mischief. The captivation was in his eyes. They were eyes of such purity and such clarity that no words needed to be spoken when he smiled. They shouted to everyone, "Welcome to my universe!" There was, however, a caveat. His eyes continued, "You're welcome as long as you understand it's *my* universe!" That law was fundamental in Blake's world. All were accepted as long as they understood *Blake's Law*.

Worlds adjoin to Blake's in order to acknowledge *Blake's Law*. They also recognize titles. Titles are appealing in those worlds, be they earned, self-pronounced, or granted. CEO, President, Director, Manager, and Boss come to mind. We often seek titles as validation. Blake's universe is different. He requires no title; his stature has earned him the right to bestow. To my remembering, although the moniker could easily have been Scoutmaster, Counselor, or Teacher, there was no greater title than "Coach." And to my remembering, there was no sweeter sound to hear than "Dad." I loved coaching the eleven- and twelve-year-old Farmington Cubs. I loved coaching my son Blake.

On that magical night, measuring 5 feet 5 inches tall with the wingspan to match, weighing 140 pounds, starting in right field for the Farmington Cubs, #9, Blake Curtis, stood at the plate in the center of his universe.

Blake had played much baseball before that magical night. His carefree attitude enabled him to become the baseball player he was. He wasn't great, but he could hit the ball. The pleasure from hitting continually brought him back. It was of no consequence that he often struck out. He loved playing baseball with the other boys. The FABL leadership had been very accepting. They openly welcomed Blake to play in their league. Playing ball with Blake, however, was not without incident. Two stand out.

Chapter Two—Counting

The first incident was infuriating, but with positive results; it led me to coach Blake's team. Blake was eleven and finishing in the Pinto (seven- and eight-year-old) Division. At the time I was coaching my older son, Tyler, and his team. Tyler was sixteen, and with the exception of one season as assistant, I had always been his coach. Blake deserved his turn, but I wanted to be with Tyler one more year. Coaching Tyler gave me the chance to be with him and show him he was also important.

The league allowed us to handpick Blake's coach while I was with Tyler. Todd Elm had agreed to take on the challenge and had done well with Blake to that point. Tyler's and Blake's games conflicted. Todd was on his own with Blake until I arrived. I finished with Tyler's team and quickly left to catch up with Blake. Blake was in the field and was happy when I joined him. There was no hint of any problem. We finished the inning and jogged toward the dugout to get ready to bat. I caught up with Todd.

"How did it go, Todd? Did Blake do well?"

Todd hesitated. His countenance exposed the internal conflict he felt as he debated his answer.

"There were issues. I'll talk to you about it later."

I would have let "issues" go, but I was worked up from Tyler's game.

"What do you mean, 'issues'? Let's talk about it *now*!"

Todd saw I was agitated.

"There were issues, but don't worry about it. I'll talk to you about it later."

I wasn't in the frame of mind for a debate as to how and why Blake should be included, but being put off made me angrier. I thought it best to walk away.

"Yeah, we'll *definitely* talk later."

I walked toward Kristi, Blake's mom and my wife, searching for calm. Todd's wife, Kathy, was keeping the game scorebook. As I passed, another of the player's moms questioned Kathy.

"Did you write down the last out Blake made?"

"It's okay. I don't have to mark it down. Blake doesn't count."

Carl Sagan wrote that the universe came into existence with one big bang. My emotions are the same. They burst forth, from a nowhere within. BANG! The universe exploded! I was furious. I didn't know what Kathy meant; I really didn't care.

"What do you mean, 'Blake doesn't count?'"

Kathy was taken aback, but she tried to keep her composure.

"We all agreed that Blake can take his turn, but he doesn't count for the team."

I lost it. "Who're 'we'? I don't remember being part of any discussion."

"You'll have to talk to Todd. It's all been worked out."

"Oh, I'll talk to Todd. But *nothing* has been worked out. This was never the deal. Blake is playing the same as everyone else!"

After the confrontation with Kathy, I had to leave. I feared I would ruin the game for everyone. It took me a couple of days to calm down. I couldn't understand what motivated "we." Blake was not the best player on the team, but he wasn't the worst either. Had I been coaching the team, he would have batted eighth in the group of twelve. There were boys on that team that hadn't hit the ball all season. Blake was on base one of every three at-bats. When I had cooled, I went to see Todd. He wasn't home, so I called him.

"Todd, don't stop me until I'm through. Just hear me out. I'm really mad about this. When we started the season, we agreed Blake would play the same rules as the other boys. If winning is so important that you and your team's parents think you're penalized when he makes an out, do what you have to do. Don't put him down in the scorebook. I don't care about the book, and I don't care about winning. It may be selfish, but I'm only there for Blake. But your wife has to be wiser. The worst thing she could ever say, in any context, is, 'Blake doesn't count.' That she said it in front of the other boys is unforgivable. Blake is smart, and so are the other boys. If you're not going to include him in the scoring, do it so Blake and the boys don't know."

Remember that in Blake's universe time is not a fixed construct. Moving from back or forth in time and returning again happens often. It happens so that everyone can understand why I act and react the way I do; it happens so that all can understand why Blake does what he does; it happens so that all can understand how Blake arrived where he is.

———

I chose Todd from among league coaches because I thought he understood our family's struggle to meet both Tyler's and Blake's needs. He was, as he should have been, focused on his own son and on winning. His and Kathy's actions evinced a lack of concern and understanding for Blake. Blake was not at the center of their world, and to them *Blake's Law* apparently did not apply. However, there have been many along the way who have supported the law, many willing to realign the heavens to serve my son.

In our church, twelve-year-old boys have opportunity to pass the sacrament, to give out the bread and the water that represent the emblems of Jesus's Last Supper. We know parents of boys with Down syndrome whose sons were given that same opportunity; we also know parents whose sons were denied. We approached our own bishop about Blake's participation well before Blake turned twelve. We felt Blake was capable, and we wanted to anticipate any confrontation in the event there were unforeseen hurdles. There were none; our bishop was loving, kind, and wise.

"Of course Blake can pass the sacrament with the other boys," Bishop Cotton said. "He's part of our congregational family. But I'm concerned about how he will do when he starts. Maybe you ought to shadow him until we are confident he can function on his own."

The day came for Blake to be sustained as a deacon before the congregation. Bishop Cotton asked me to sit on the stand with Blake while everyone voted in acceptance. The vote was not out of the ordinary. Every twelve-year-old boy who becomes a deacon stands before the entire congregation to be sustained by a show of hands. As I waited with Blake for the bishop to call him, I gently reminded him.

"Remember to raise your hand too."

There was an unusually large group gathered. I watched Blake carefully as he pulled on his tie. It was a new tie that Kristi bought just for the occasion. It was bright and colorful, and it matched perfectly with his light brown suit, although it was mostly hidden beneath his jacket. It was his first real necktie. We had finally advanced from clip-on ties to the real thing. Perhaps it was too soon for that tie. Sitting in front of that many people made the tie seem too tight. When the bishop called Blake forward, he refused to stand at the pulpit. The tie seemed to loosen as I quietly whispered to Blake.

"It's okay, Blakey. I'll go stand with you."

I always smile when I think about the introduction. As we stood together, Bishop Cotton turned with Blake to the congregation.

"Everyone, this is Blake Curtis."

Bishop Cotton was wonderful, but Blake has made sure everyone already knows who he is. This is, after all, his world. Typically when introduced, a young boy will do nothing more than acknowledge the congregation with a nod or a smile. Blake gave a shy smile, paused, and then turned and faced the crowd. His suit jacket opened, exposing his bright new tie, and he gave a huge wave. It was as if the sun had broken through the clouds. His sincerity and spontaneity shouted, "Look, everyone, it's me, and I can do this!" We all laughed with great pleasure. In that instant I tried to slip unnoticed back into my own seat. The moment wasn't about me; it was about Blake. He was aware of my every move. When he sensed me pull away, he panicked. He pulled on his jacket, covering his new tie. I had to quickly return. He immediately calmed; his jacket opened again.

Bishop Cotton continued. "Blake has been interviewed and has been found worthy to be sustained as a deacon. Will all those willing to accept and support him please raise their hand?" All raised their hands, and I felt a rush of emotion. Blake was also caught in the moment. He forgot to vote for himself. The bishop looked toward Blake.

"Raise your hand too, Blakey."

Much to everyone's delight, shyly and tightly, Blake slowly raised his hand. He smiled, and everyone laughed again. These are the moments that keep me going. We all seek acceptance and understanding. Every father dreams about his children's successes before their birth. All of us hope for an Olympian, for a future president, or for a Rhodes scholar. The birth of a child with disability brings those dreams crashing down. When he was born, I didn't know if Blake would walk; I didn't know if Blake would talk; I didn't know if Blake would learn to read and write. Then, through the healing process, realization of the joy for the child to just *be* rolls forth. The smallest progression, the simplest genesis, brings satisfaction and light. Now, twelve years later, thanks to a kind and loving bishop, Blake would pass the sacrament with all the other boys. He would fulfill his spiritual duty. I knew with whom Blake counted.

———

When Todd was finally able to respond, to answer whether or not Blake counted, he wasn't very good at consolation. But perhaps he had been paying attention to those who supported Blake.

"We've already talked about Blake, and what to do."

There was that mysterious *we* again. When I was young and retreated to the *we* defense, my dad would ask, "Who is 'we'? Do you have a mouse in your pocket?" I really wanted to know who *we* were and how *we* had somehow claimed authority.

"We were wrong," Todd continued. "You and I agreed before the season started how Blake would play. There's no reason to change. Can we forget about it and move on?"

It was *counting* that set me off. Kathy didn't intend to suggest that Blake wasn't important in the universe, but my inference wasn't exaggerated. Leaving him out of the scorebook implied that Blake was worth less. Todd didn't offer any more details. I never discovered what the "issues" were, and I was never privy to who "we" were. I let it go. I let go to the extent I recognized if Blake were to have opportunity, I needed to coach his team. The season finished without any more trouble. Then I faced Tyler.

"Tyler, I've been able to coach your team for ten years. It's Blake's turn."

That was the only explanation I gave. Perhaps I should have been more specific. There is no universal manual for raising children with Down syndrome, and there is no universal manual for raising siblings of children with Down syndrome. Being a sibling of a child with Down syndrome must be incredibly difficult, especially when you are surrounded. Tyler's older sister Amanda, whose name appropriately means *worthy to be loved*, is also Down syndrome. Amanda and Blake have a natural defense, a shield that protects them from understanding ridicule. Tyler does not have that same shield. Quite often, away from the safety of home, he has been the recipient of insults that are directed at his siblings and him. Amanda and Blake have naturally received attention; Tyler has had to fight for every bit of attention he receives in the community.

Somehow he understood. I love Tyler, and I'm grateful for his sacrifice.

Chapter Three—Accommodation

The second incident came more as a backhanded compliment than a complaint. Blake was twelve and on his way to the Farmington Mustang (nine- and ten-year-old) Division. As the season neared, I called the league to see what could be done to help Blake succeed. The Pinto Division used a pitching machine instead of a live pitcher. Blake had mastered hitting the ball with the machine to the extent there was fear for opposing players. He was getting bigger and stronger, and the bases in the Pinto Division were very close. When he hit the ball hard, it moved, and the possibility he would rocket the ball down the third baseline toward an unprotected boy was real. We had to try something different, but I was concerned about Blake's reaction when he faced a real pitcher. What would he do when standing eye-to-eye with someone who was intentionally trying to strike him out? I pondered the situation, and then I offered a proposal to the league.

"Tim, would it be all right if I pitched to Blake during league games?"

Tim Markinson, the league president, considered.

"We want Blake to play," he answered. "But I'm afraid if you pitched, the game would slow down too much. It would disrupt the flow and rhythm."

Tim wasn't trying to exclude Blake. He just wanted to make sure everyone had a positive experience. After reconsidering, I offered an alternative.

"How about this, Tim? Can we modify the strike zone for Blakey?"

Tim was intrigued. "Go on," he said.

"Blake will swing at any pitch. When pitchers figure out he swings at everything, striking him out will be too easy. How about a rule that the only pitch called a strike on Blakey is a pitch that is actually in the strike zone? If the pitch is in the dirt and Blake swings, the pitch will be called a ball. If the pitch is three feet above his head and he swings, the pitch will still be a ball. Only pitches in the strike zone will be strikes, and they will be strikes whether he swings or not. When he runs the bases, he'll play just the same as everyone else."

Tim didn't hesitate. "That sounds fair." All of the other coaches in the league were notified, and all agreed to the *Blake Rule*. There was no issue with the *Blake Rule* until the late season. Blake's team's name was the Angels, and Blake had hit well, being a regular contributor to the Angels' success. As the end-of-season tournament approached, the standings were close, and every team in the league was looking for any advantage to pick up more wins. Such scrutiny can find us gazing into each other's world. In *A Tale of Two Cities*, Charles Dickens considered closely held secrets within those worlds:

> A wonderful fact to reflect upon, that every human creature is constituted to be that profound secret and mystery to every other. A solemn consideration, when I enter a great city by night, that every one of those darkly clustered houses encloses its own secret; that every room in every one of them encloses its own secret; that every beating heart in the hundreds of thousands of breasts there

is, in some of its imaginings, a secret to the heart nearest it![3]

It is difficult to peer into a man's heart and understand his imaginings. All men possess hidden secrets that our gaze cannot penetrate. Motive is difficult to interpret without knowing those secrets and often remains a mystery. I don't pretend to understand why men do what they do, but I often wonder. I try to see; I hope they seek.

———

As I try to see, as I consider my own motives, a stare received can be quite revealing; it can hold the key to unlocking my own profound secrets and mysteries. I've returned many stares, both kind and cruel. They are easily distinguished.

We took the entire family to a restaurant for dinner. We trailed the hostess as she walked us toward our table. Amanda was excited and anxious; she was immediately behind. I watched the eyes of a female patron open a bit as she passed. Then, as Tigger would follow Pooh, Blake bounced behind his sister. He was on his never-ending quest to always be first. When the woman caught sight of him, her eyes became huge. She refused to look away. There were no audible words. There was no need. Her stare screamed her contempt. I couldn't let it go. I leaned to her as I drew near.

"Yes, we really do have two of them!"

Startled, she shrugged and quickly turned away. She was humiliated. She pretended to have neither looked nor heard what I said. Her gaze was cruel and empty. It reconfirmed within me my own love for both Amanda and Blake. Love is a powerful motivator.

———

3   Charles Dickens, *A Tale of Two Cities*, (Mineola, NY: Dover, 1999), 8.

As other men seek, their insight into Blake's world is not as clear. Blake's team was scheduled to play the Red Sox. Before the game, their assistant coach approached our team scorekeeper, Clint Harris.

"Excuse me. Are you familiar with the rule you use for the *boy* on your team?"

"Pardon me?"

The question was opaque. Of course Clint knew which *boy* the assistant was referring to, but he didn't know which direction the conversation would turn.

"You know. The special rule you use for the *boy* on your team."

"You mean the boy on our team with Down syndrome?"

"Yes, he's the one. We've decided we're not going to use that rule today."

We were back! Just who were *we*? Had Todd and Kathy called a meeting and *we* were all invited? *We* had developed a worldwide design I wasn't aware of.

Clint paused. He wasn't sure what to do.

"Do you see the man standing with *the boy* over there?" he said, pointing to Blakey and me. "He's the coach of our team. He's also *the boy's* father. Why don't you ask him?"

The assistant acted on Clint's suggestion. He boldly approached.

"Are you the coach of the Angels?"

"Yes. What can I do for you?" At the time I had no idea what the man wanted.

"The special rule you use for that boy on your team? We're not going to use it today." The man wasn't asking a question. He declared his intention, and I bristled at his tone.

"Stop right there," I snapped back. "Let's clear up a few things before you go any further and say something you may regret. That *boy* you're talking about is my son. As for the rule, what rule are you talking about?" His questions were now transparent. I knew perfectly well the rule to which the man referred, but I was irritated. I wanted to force him to verbalize it.

"The strike zone rule. We're not going to use it today."

"Yes, *we* are. The rule was approved by the league president and every coach at the beginning of the season. There's no reason to change now."

"But it's not fair!" he whined. "It gives your team an unfair advantage!"

This was unexpected—a bit of a cosmic shift! Blake had now moved from not counting to unfair advantage! He had traveled halfway around the universe, light-years from where he began. I laughed out loud. Blake Curtis, the only player with Down syndrome to ever play in the FABL, was an unfair advantage! I couldn't believe what I was hearing. That Blake was considered a legitimate player was clear; that he was considered an unfair advantage was cloudy. What secret did this man hold in his heart? It seemed he saw Blake through cataracts.

"Do you understand why we put the rule in place?"

"Sure, so the boy would have opportunity to succeed. But I've watched the boy. He can hit the ball. The rule gives him an unfair advantage. The chance he'll strike out is nonexistent."

It was shocking, even a little exhilarating, that anyone considered Blake, with or without a modified strike zone, an unfair advantage for our team. I answered without thinking.

"Of course the rule was put in place to help Blake succeed. It's the entire point! As to Blake striking out, you apparently don't understand the rule. He can strike out. He has many times."

It bothered me I had to justify Blake striking out. I continued in not as gentle a tone.

"I told you, the rule was approved by everyone involved in the league before the season started. If you want to protest the game, go right ahead. But for now we're going to play with the accommodation everyone agreed to. That's the end of it."

I left the man and went to finish preparing the Angels. As I later pondered the incident, I realized what respect the man had shown for Blakey. His implication was that Blake could play the game as well as any other boy without rule changes. Although I was angry at the time, upon reflection, there was no need to carry the anger. Blake was paid a great compliment, even if it was backhanded.

———

That man—I never learned his name—must have watched Blake closely during the season to draw his conclusions. I was surprised at the attention he paid to Blake, although I shouldn't have been. Blake had played well that season and continued to improve. In an earlier game, he hit the ball far. I was standing in the third-base coach's box at the time. I was distracted and looked up just in time to see him make contact. His swing was sweet; he hit the ball so hard it flew over the center fielder's head. The small crowd roared their approval. Blake stood motionless as he admired the hit. I brought him back to earth.

"Run, Blakey! Run to first base!"

He looked over to me and smiled. He dropped his bat and ran for first. Blake is not a fast runner. The ball carried far enough to be a home run for any other player in the league, but Blake was just learning to run the bases, and he had wasted precious time watching the ball's flight. He made it safely to first, and then he stopped. He had never hit well enough for the chance of an extra base. First base was the edge of the earth. Our first-base coach urged him on to uncharted territory at second. When he finally made it to second, the fielder had tracked down the ball. We probably could have coaxed him to third, but I didn't want to risk his being thrown out and ruining the moment.

I remembered Blake standing happily at second base. I remembered standing in the third-base coach's box, ecstatic over his success. The gazes from the crowd were surprised and admiring. I wondered if that hit were the basis for the charge that Blake had an unfair advantage.

———

Blake came to the plate soon after the debate over the *Blake Rule*. I had hoped he would have his best game ever. I was still seething over the confrontation before the game. There was no advantage. The Farmington Mustang league was the major leagues for Blake. Every other boy in the league would have opportunity to continue on, to aspire to being a major leaguer. This was perhaps as far in baseball as Blake would go.

I was looking for another mammoth blow as Blake readied for the at-bat. Unfortunately, his first plate appearance was a short one. He struck out quickly. It was difficult to be pleased by my son's strikeout, but it proved a point. Fortunately, it was a starting point. Blake came to the plate three more times that game. He hit the ball hard every time and ended with three base hits in four at-bats. Each of his hits was timely. There were always runners aboard the bases, and they consequently scored each time he made contact with the ball. He had five RBIs for the day and scored three runs himself.

From Blake's universe, I watched turmoil in another. The man grew angrier with each of Blake's hits. His emotions reached their apex when Blake connected for his third hit of the game. He grabbed a bat and slammed it against the pole of the dugout fence. I took pleasure in his anger. There had never been a time I let myself even hope Blake could generate that reaction at a baseball game. The Angels won the game handily, winning, in great measure, because of Blake's contribution. At the game's conclusion, the teams both gathered near home plate. I offered my hand to the man in a gesture of sportsmanship. He tersely refused and stormed away. There would be no contact between our worlds. I wondered what could drive a man into a hole of such bitterness.

Chapter Four—Rhythm

A new league president, Ryan West, was put in place during the off-season. As the new season approached, Ryan, along with the rest of the league, agreed to allow the *Blake Rule* again. The beginning of every new season renewed my dreams of Blakey playing in a championship game. I secretly hoped the title game would come down to one last at-bat, with Blakey delivering the game-winning hit. I wasn't any different from the parents of the boys I coached. We all held that same hope. The dream was perhaps a stretch when considering Blake. It should have been enough for me just to see him play.

Our team, the Cubs, played well through the season. The Cubs' record was 8–4, good enough for second place. The team's solid play continued into the postseason tournament. On the dawn of that magical day, only three teams were left in the double-elimination brackets. Both the Cubs and the Dodgers had lost one game. They would play each other first. The winner would play the Rays for the championship.

The day that held the magical night began as any other. I pulled my 5-foot-11, slightly overweight frame out of bed. I ran the water unnecessarily long in the shower to warm it. Next, I needlessly applied shampoo to my hairless head. Its application was my guilty pleasure, the consequence of adult male-pattern baldness. Why do bald men use shampoo? I continued my morning routine by clipping my lip so deeply while shaving it wouldn't stop bleeding.

Finally, I climbed into the car for the morning commute. I typically got up early on game day to plan the lineup for the evening's play, but on this day there was no need. I knew which boys would be to the game, and I planned on using the same lineup as in the previous loss to the league-leading Rays. The struggle was finding a way to help the Cubs prepare for another game.

Perhaps time is relative in my universe. Through the course of the daylong struggle to prepare, much of the baseball I enjoyed throughout my life ran together. I remembered the game I played as a boy. I remembered warm summer afternoons spent with my friends, throwing and hitting the ball, growing up as boys ought to grow. I pondered the game I loved as a man. I pondered its beauty and prose, played out in stadiums by men, played as though they were still boys. I dreamed about the game I coached as a father. I dreamed of my boy, throwing and hitting the ball, becoming more of a man than I ever thought possible. It came to me. It's about the rhythm of the game.

The Rhythm of the Game? How do you explain the rhythm of the game to a twelve-year-old? How do you explain the rhythm of the game to anyone? Earlier I had talked indirectly about rhythm to the boys. It was now clear they didn't understand. I considered a different approach to help the message resonate.

———

The earlier event in the instructive must not have been clear. We take infield as each practice begins. The players go to their positions to catch ground balls, finishing each fielding chance with a timely throw to first. Unfortunately, the routine had become monotonous. As we wrapped up the drill on a warm afternoon, Sky Simpson, the inquisitor, questioned out loud.

"Why do we always take infield during practice? Why not just choose teams and play a game?"

In Sky's world, the sun was peaking over the horizon. He was questioning! Twelve is a wonderful age for boys. Twelve-year-old boys suddenly want to know why. I'd been searching for a way to help the boys become a team, and Sky gave me an opening. Although I wasn't sure how to answer his question, I didn't want to miss the opportunity. I didn't know if Sky were prepared for the sun's full light, so I was cautious. I smiled to him as I charted the course of the discussion.

"We get better by doing the same thing over and over. We work each time to make it perfect. It becomes habit. Then, when the time comes that it matters, when we're playing in a real game, we know exactly what to do without thinking. We don't have to decide. Together, as a team, we already know what to do."

I paused while he reflected. Then I spoke to all the boys.

"Should we work on something different? Sky wants to play a game. Let's play a game called Hot-Box."

We gathered at first base. I divided the boys into two groups. The first group stood at first behind Justin Farmer. I moved between the bags as the other group followed Jared Wise to second. Jared Wise was a great infielder. He didn't say much; he was quiet and shy, but his on-the-field play spoke volumes. He seldom missed a catch. He just needed confidence. He needed someone else to see that he was great, and he needed to feel he was part of the team.

"All right, gentlemen. Here we go."

Baseball is timeless. The game endures; it is passed from father to son. Sure, there are elements that are generationally adapted, but the game's fundamentals are the same. In the game's beginnings, when a runner was caught between two bases, he was in a rundown. Then, when I was a boy, we called it a hot-box. Today, boys call it a pickle. No matter what you call it, it is the same, and it is a fundamental baseball play. It is also a great activity to forge a team out of twelve individual boys.

I stood between the bases. Justin started with the ball at first base. He ran toward me, forcing me to second. When Justin realized he couldn't reach me to tag me out, he threw the ball to Jared at second. Justin kept running without the ball, moving past me to second base, taking his place in line behind the others. Jared caught the ball and chased me back toward first. Seth Pollard took Justin's place in the front of the line at first base. Jared pinched me toward Seth and threw the ball. Without the ball, Jared ran past me to take his place behind the others at first. Chase Everett stepped in behind him at second and got ready for a throw from Seth. The rundown's weave continued. Over, then under; over, then under. Jared Wise worked to the front of the line at first base. He ran toward me with the ball, and as I collapsed, he tagged me out. We laughed and laughed. The boys had mastered the rundown's weave. They felt its rhythm.

The Cubs were spontaneously learning the joy of baseball. Each team member understood his role. Although in a single moment only one boy could actually hold the ball, the team, the entire team, acted as baseball's trinity. They held the ball, they threw the ball, and they caught the ball together as each took his turn. Before the rundown began, we were I; we were me. When Jared Wise tagged me out, me became we.

"We got you!"

Everyone played his part. Chase Everett, Davey Strait, Seth Pollard, Justin Farmer, Blake Curtis, Jared Wise, Sky Simpson, Johnny Coates, Buck Spalding, Collin Bose, Tony Jacobson, and Pete Henderson were now the Cubs. Twelve boys; one team. Repetition is rhythm. Repetition is practice. Repetition brings harmony to the worlds, a place for everyone.

———

Magnificently, the boys had become a team. Sadly, although they felt the rhythm, there was more to comprehend. I considered the dilemma as I arrived at the park and gathered the Cubs for their infield warm-up. Rhythm needed to be taught in a different context. I considered a more direct approach.

"Gentlemen," I said, rubbing my evening shadow with a callused hand as I addressed the team. I enjoyed referring to the boys collectively as *gentlemen*. I felt the reference raised their awareness of who they were. "Gentlemen," I asked again, this time pulling off my worn and soiled cap and rubbing my balding but well-shampooed head, "why do you think we lost our last game?" There was no tone of accusation. I only hoped to use the moment to teach the boys.

There was a pause; then one of the boys answered.

"We lost because we weren't ready to play," blurted out Buck Spalding, the football player turned third baseman. Buck, small for a football player, was *the fastest of them all* and was the most respectful boy I ever had coached.

The other boys then joined in and gave their reasons for the loss. The explanations were what I expected from twelve-year-old boys, but none were what I perceived as the reason for the loss. I seized the opportunity to explain *the rhythm of the game.*

"Gentlemen, have any of you ever played basketball?" The boys looked puzzled, but most of them raised their hands and nodded their heads yes.

"When you play basketball, have you ever had a game when every shot you threw at the basket went in?" Without waiting for a reply, I continued. "When that's how you feel, what do you want?"

There was another pause; then Pete Henderson shouted it out.

"I want the ball!"

Pete was the *baller* on the team. He was not the best athlete of the group, but he was definitely the best baseball player. Pete loved to play. His wisdom of the game, and the world in general, far surpassed the understanding of most twelve-year-olds.

"You want the ball!" I echoed. "That's right! You feel good. You know when you shoot the ball, it will go in the basket. You can just feel it. The game comes to you. Baseball is no different; when you feel the rhythm of the game, it comes to you. The shortstop wants to field the ball. The cleanup hitter wants to hit the ball. The pitcher wants to pitch the ball."

The discussion was subtly directed toward one of the Cubs' pitchers, Seth Pollard. Seth, a handsome boy of twelve, pitched in the previous loss. He was lean and rangy, a terrific boy, and a terrific athlete. But he was not beautiful because of his athletic ability; rather, he was beautiful because of his untainted guilelessness. Unfortunately, he did not understand rhythm. Much of the reason for the loss was that Seth had struggled on the mound, searching for, but never finding, his rhythm.

I pulled the boys closer in anticipation of sending them to the field.

"All right, gentlemen," I said, "let's go to the field and learn what rhythm is. Remember, rhythm doesn't mean fast, but it doesn't mean slow either. Rhythm is your mind and body working together at the right pace in order to reach your goal. Rhythm is the team working together to move the game in the right direction. Rhythm is flow."

I stood on the pitcher's mound and spoke one more time.

"Gentlemen, I'll be the pitcher striking out the batter. Once the third strike is thrown, who starts throwing the ball 'around the horn'?"

"The catcher!" a few of the boys shouted together.

The plan was working. The boys put the painful loss out of their minds and were remembering the joys of the game. I threw the ball to the catcher. The catcher, in turn, rose up and rifled the ball to third. The ball followed its course "around the horn" to second, then to short, and then to first.

It wasn't perfect. For a while, the Farmington Cubs looked more like the *Bad News Bears*. The second basemen threw the ball to first rather than to shortstop. The shortstop dropped the ball. The first baseman wasn't paying attention. But slowly the beat penetrated. The boys began to catch, to raise, and to throw, in succession.

All in flow; all in rhythm.

I sought to help Seth. I hoped the exercise would solve the rhythm problem and put the entire team on track. Rhythm is the most challenging concept for boys to understand in a sporting event. It is even more difficult for a grown man to teach. When the drill was finished, I walked toward the dugout to fill out the lineup card. I bumped into Ted Thompson, coach of the Rays. Ted was a great baseball tactician. He had successfully coached boys in Little League for many seasons. He was also the coach of the all-star team, a team on which Seth had earned a place. He struck up a conversation.

"I saw Seth today, and I worked with him on his mechanics. He seemed to struggle in the last game, and I wanted to help."

"Thanks, Ted. I saw he was out of sync too. I'm not sure, though, if his problem is mechanical. We worked on trying to reestablish his rhythm."

Ted's diagnosis wasn't too different from mine; rhythm and mechanics are closely related. A successful pitcher has both working together. The different approaches to solving the problem, however, were striking. The components to successful coaching at any level of sport, and in any sport, are, first, teaching fundamentals; second, managing the game; and third, reading the players. The hierarchy of these components varies from coach to coach. Ted chose to correct Seth's problem by going with his strength, teaching fundamentals. I opted to address Seth's issue another way. Fundamentals are critical to success, but to me, understanding boys is paramount.

In his book, *The Elements of Style*, William Strunk wrote:

The first principle of composition, therefore, is to forsee or determine the shape of what is to come and pursue that shape.

A sonnet is built on a fourteen-line frame, each line containing five feet. Hence, sonneteers know exactly where they are headed, although they may not know how to get there. Most forms of composition are less clearly defined, more flexible, but all have skeletons to which the writer will bring the flesh and the blood. The more clearly the writer perceives the shape, the better are the chances of success.[4]

Strunk could have written that baseball is like a sonnet. There is rhythm to a team's composition that allows a coach to express his thoughts artfully. Coaches who build great baseball teams build them by teaching fundamentals. That is the shape they perceive. I wanted to build great men. I chose baseball as the tool to instruct the concepts of the universe. The tool doesn't have to be baseball. Maybe it's art. Perhaps it's music or even mathematics. Ted's focus was to make sure that Seth held the baseball properly, raised the baseball properly, and let go of the baseball properly. He saw the shape of what was to come as he instructed Seth toward baseball success. Perhaps there was greater opportunity, however, while giving Seth instruction; perhaps there was opportunity for shaping a boy into more than a baseball player.

The shape of what is to come is determined as order is established from chaos. The wonder of being with boys lies in playing a role in that definition. The shape has disorganized beginnings, and it is not brought into focus by an accidental process. Changes in boys are not random. A guiding hand is required. For ballplayers, dropped balls, bad throws, and strikeouts must be replaced with

---

4   William Strunk Jr. and E.B. White, *The Elements of Style*, 4th ed. (Needham Heights, MA. Allen and Bacon, 2000), 15.

caught balls, great throws, and base hits. For boys, tussled locks, rumpled shirts, and muddy feet are replaced with well-combed hair, well-pressed suits, and well-shined shoes. Rough-and-tumble boys become great men by design.

As the team practiced, each boy took his turn fielding grounders. For every boy, it is the same. The ball rolls between his legs; it bounces over his head; it drops from his glove. Then, as fear is replaced with confidence, each boy, in turn, knocks the ball down before it can escape through his legs. He anticipates the ball's hop before the ball flies by. He holds onto the ball with both hands. His finest hour is concentrated in learning to take a ground ball to his chest. It hurts, but it only hurts for a moment. He realizes as he keeps the ball in front there is always time to recover and make the throw to first. The boys were learning to keep the ball in front, to relax, and to enjoy the effortless, routine, disciplined throw to first base. The shape of what was to come had been determined and pursued. Its composition was about more than just baseball.

Chapter Five—Signs

I finished the conversation with Ted and turned in my lineup. There was time to gather the team once more to go over game signs. The nonverbal hand motions I used to communicate with the boys had worked well. I hadn't always used the signs. When Blake moved from the Pinto Division to the Mustang Division, however, I was afraid it might be the last season he would play, and probably my last season as coach. I didn't know if nine-year-olds were capable of using baseball signs, but I decided to try. If it were going to be my last season, I wanted to teach everything I could to see if it would work.

The signs were successful, even with nine-year-olds. All the boys learned them, including Blake. Although I didn't realize it at the time, he had learned each sign and knew what each meant. He was home with Kristi after an evening game; he pulled her aside to show her his newly obtained baseball knowledge.

"Mom, I show you the signs."

"What signs, Blakey? What are you talking about?"

Blake was aggravated. It was his universe. Based upon that ownership, Blake regularly assumed anyone he talked to knew whom, and what, he was talking about.

"Mom, the baseball signs!"

Kristi had no idea what signs he was talking about, but she understood Blake as only a mother can. She went with it.

"Okay, Blake, show me the signs."

Blake went over each signal with her. He was perfect. When I came home, Kristi asked me about the signs.

"Are you using signals for baseball this year?"

"Yes. I wasn't sure the nine-year-olds would pick them up, but it has worked out pretty well. Why ?"

"Have you taught them to Blake?"

"Yes and no. He's always with the team when I go over them, but I haven't singled him out."

"Well, he's learned them all. He showed them to me."

It was a great victory. I had no idea he understood. I had assumed a limit that did not exist in his world. He was far more capable than I knew. I recommitted to Blake's universe. There would be no deviation from *Blake's Law*. He would set his own boundaries. After that day, whenever we gathered the team to go over the signs, Blake became the teacher.

As I looked to gather the Cubs and go over the signs, I searched for Blake. I had been so caught up in conversation with Ted and with turning in the lineup that I had lost track of him. Blake generally stayed close; from time to time, however, he sneaked away to pursue his own agenda. I panicked. The present became the past in my universe.

———

I recalled an incident from Scout camp. We were halfway through the week and were having the best time. But it had been taxing. I had purposely been with Blake twenty-four hours a day for those three days. Taking a boy with Down syndrome into the wilderness isn't easy, and I was uncomfortable leaving him with anyone else, but I needed an hour to recharge. Blake was tired and had slipped into the tent to take a short nap. I looked for Charlie Mortensen, the assistant scoutmaster, and asked for help.

"Charlie, can you keep an eye on Blakey for a while? I just need to get away for a minute."

"Sure, I'd be glad to help. Where is he?"

When Blake was younger, he regularly tried to sneak away. As he matured, he didn't seek out adventure as often, but from time to time it still happened. When Charlie asked where Blake was, he gave me opportunity for a little more explanation.

"He's in our tent sleeping. But it is really important you check on him. If he wakes up and I'm not there, he'll go looking for me."

"That won't be a problem. I'll keep an eye on him."

I worried. I'd been through this before when I asked for help watching Blake. Understanding how closely Blake had to be watched was seldom understood.

"I'm not trying to be pushy, but you have to know where he is *all the time*. He can sneak away in a flash, without anyone knowing."

I still wasn't sure Charlie completely understood. He assured me he was capable, so I left. I returned about an hour later and went to the tent to check on Blake. He wasn't there. I looked for Charlie.

"Charlie, have you seen Blake?"

"Yes. He's in your tent. I just checked."

I went back and checked one more time. Blake was gone. I was alarmed. The Yellowstone wilderness is huge. The forest looks the same in every direction. One hundred yards from a trail might just as well be one hundred miles from a trail. Where did he go? I had to find him! I didn't know what I would do if Blake were lost. I'd read stories about children with disabilities being lost in the wilderness. None of those stories ended well.

I collected myself and considered where he may have gone. Blake never wanders anywhere. He does not travel aimlessly. When he sets out on his own, he has purpose. I thought of all the places we had been in the past few days. I set off east down the trail toward the waterfront. We had gone swimming and boating on Monday. Blake wasn't there. Then I headed south around the lake. That trail led to a natural spring. Again, no luck.

With each passing minute, my concern inched closer to a full-blown panic. I ran back to camp with the plan of heading west to the rifle range when I met my good friend Jed Bush, the camp director.

"Are you looking for something?"

Blake peeked shyly from behind Jed. I hadn't seen him until that moment. He was afraid he was in trouble. I was just happy to see him safe.

"Where did you go, Blakey?"

"I look for you."

I was happy to have Blake back, safe. I owe a great debt of gratitude to the camp staff and to Jed. Jed knows Blakey quite well. I had explained Blakey's pursuits to him on several occasions; I warned him about Blakey's travels well before we went to camp so that Jed could prepare. He understood my seriousness when I told him, "If you ever see Blake without me, assume that I don't know where he is."

In anticipation of Blake's visit to camp, Jed had relayed that information to his staff. Jed's staffers had inadvertently stumbled upon Blakey as he walked west, toward the rifle range. We'd spent the previous afternoon there together. The young men on the camp staff handled Blake brilliantly. When the staff members bumped into him, they knew just what to do. Blake was on the trail but was ready to walk into the forest in search of me. Before he could leave the trail, the more experienced Scouts questioned him.

"Hi, Blake! How are you?"

Blake smiled his devilish smile, looked back over both shoulders as if someone were standing behind him, and then pointed to himself.

"You mean me?"

"Sure! Do you like camping? Where are you going?"

"I love camping. I looking for my dad. You seen him?"

"No. We don't know where he is. But come with us, and we'll help you find him"

I'm so grateful for those young men. They understood what Blake did not. They were smart enough to know how dangerous it was for Blake to search for someone in the forest by himself. Those great young men helped Blake avoid trouble. Blake's world is full of great young men.

Chapter Six—Barriers

Even with as well as those young men handled Blake, I still always worried when he sneaked away. I didn't know if he would always be surrounded by such fine young men. I could never completely relax unless I was certain where he was. This time I found Blake with the team. The boys were sitting in a loose circle, bemoaning the pain of Mrs. Johnson's English class. Blake hadn't had the pleasure of Mrs. Johnson, but he was included in the conversation. He snickered and played with the team as they talked. He grabbed Collin Bose's hat and ran away, enjoying his version of tag. Collin was great with Blake. He chased Blake playfully. After he retrieved his hat, he grabbed Blake's. Blake cackled as he chased Collin, finally snatching back his own hat. With cap in hand, he looked toward Seth. Seth had playfully turned his own cap sideways. Blake mimicked him. They both laughed and laughed.

"C'mon, Blake," I said when they were through. "Let's get everyone together in the dugout and go over the signs."

Sky jumped to his feet. "Hey, everyone, Blake is going to show us the signs. Let's go."

Everyone followed to the dugout. Blake stood in front of the team with his back turned to the Dodgers. The boys gave him their full attention.

"Blake, what does 'indicator' mean?" I asked.

"Sign before the sign."

"Very good. What is the indicator sign?"

"You pull on your ear."

"That's right. What do I do when I want you to steal?"

"You move your hand across your chest, like this."

———

I've worked to understand Blake's abilities in order to mentor his progress. Blake is capable, but there are times when parameters, such as the *Blake Rule* for the strike zone, should be changed to help him succeed. Although there have been many along the way willing to facilitate adjustments, sometimes it takes a little prodding. I went to the deacons quorum leader, Randy Wilson, as Blake prepared to pass the sacrament for the first time.

"Randy, I've been thinking about Blake. Can I offer a few suggestions that might help when he passes the bread and water?"

"Don't worry about it, Jeff. We'll take care of it."

"Hear me out on this, Randy. Blake is routine oriented. He'll get confused if you have him go to a different spot in the chapel each week when he helps. He'll do better if you have him always go to the same benches. Those benches should be on the side of the chapel with the wall. Then, when the tray reaches the wall, it will be passed back to Blake. If Blake passes a tray to a pew that has an aisle on each side, he'll be confused. He won't understand that the deacon at the other end of the bench will send it back on the next row. He'll walk all the way around to the other side of the pew to pick up his tray rather than just stepping back one row and waiting for the tray to come back."

"Don't worry about it, Jeff. We'll take care of it."

I am grateful for Randy; he took personal interest in Blake. He always treated Blakey well. I was, however, still a little skeptical about depending on someone else to help Blake succeed, and Randy had his own learning curve with Blake. As I had warned, Blake got confused when he passed the sacrament to different places, and he struggled with the tray exchange. Randy finally approached me.

"Jeff, I've been thinking. Blake would probably do better if we had him pass the sacrament to the same benches every week. Plus, I think the tray exchange confuses him. Maybe he should pass the sacrament on the side of the chapel where the benches line the wall. That way he'll always get his same tray back."

I needed to let go. It was difficult. Then it came to me. It didn't matter whose idea it was. Randy was willing to help. He *wanted* to help. If it made Blake's success possible, I wouldn't say anything. It wouldn't be easy, but I'd keep my mouth shut. Randy was Blake's ally. He had already shown his allegiance to Blake. Through the process, Randy had wisely enlisted the help of all the boys. He assigned one of Blake's peers to shadow Blake if he got confused. He instructed another to make a map for all the boys to clarify the new routine. Blake is currently only one merit badge from earning his Eagle Scout. Much of the credit for that achievement belongs to Randy. I knew all this, but I couldn't completely purge the sarcasm from my voice when I answered.

"Those are great ideas, Randy. Thanks!"

———

We continued through the signals. The boys listened intently as Blake mimed each in succession. Then it was time to play.

Davey Strait started as pitcher for the Cubs. I had misjudged Davey's ability as a pitcher, thinking he was a year away from standing on the mound, lacking in experience and maturity. However, within two weeks of the playoffs, Chase Everett, a southpaw, the team's shortstop and number two pitcher, gave notice the Cubs would need someone else to pitch.

"Coach," Chase recited, "our team is playing so well, and I'm excited. It's too bad I won't be here for the playoffs. I love playing in the tournament, but I'm going out of town with my family."

Although disappointed Chase would be gone, we were glad he gave us enough time to get someone else ready to pitch. I chose Davey.

Every Little League team has at least one boy who desperately wants to pitch. Just as a new Lab puppy tugging at and refusing to let go of a dishtowel, the boy constantly tugs at the shirttail of the coach, begging for an opportunity to stand on the mound. And just as the new puppy owner who tires of the game long before the dog, the coach looks for an end to the battle. I'd seen the tussle many times. My oldest son had once been mired in this struggle. Tyler's coach had devastated him and nearly destroyed his love for baseball. He had tired of the shirttail-tugging game; he purposely sent Tyler to pitch at a point when he knew Tyler would fail.

"See!" he shouted as Tyler stood on the mound, both physically and metaphorically alone after having walked several batters. "I told you that you couldn't pitch! Now go back to the dugout, and don't ever bother me about pitching again."

I suppose the man was looking to shape baseball players and to win games. We picked up the pieces and moved on. Tyler continued to play and became quite successful. I silently committed I would never be guilty of what I watched unfold that afternoon.

Davey tugged and tugged at the towel. "Coach, when will it be my turn to pitch?" His turn had come, and it was my responsibility to make sure he succeeded. He didn't disappoint. He pitched well at the end of the season and into the playoffs. I regretted not seeing his ability sooner. A good coach ought to be able to spot and to develop baseball talent.

The team scorekeeper, Bob Henderson, Pete Henderson's dad, had penciled in the visiting Dodgers' lineup along with the home team Cubs. The game was about to begin.

Davey appeared imposing as he stood on the mound. His fiery red hair belied his gentle personality. To be successful, a pitcher needs to be the biggest jerk on the diamond. The pitcher's mere presence on the mound must embody intimidation. Davey's laid-back nature initially steered me away from having him pitch. I don't always see the broader view of the universe. For all that red hair, Davey was passive and happy-go-lucky; he had a tendency to smile too much when he threw the ball. A pitcher should never give a happy smile to a batter. Still, this was Davey's day, and Davey looked comfortable from the start. His fastball was working, and he retired the first three hitters he faced without any trouble, smiling and enjoying every pitch.

———

As Davey stood on the mound that magical day, I remembered an earlier game, the first time he had pitched for the Cubs. As we prepared, we worked on holding the ball; we worked on raising the ball; we worked on letting the ball go. The real focus of the instruction had been confidence. Armed with that confidence, Davey was ready. Game day for that earlier contest arrived. Davey's dad, Ken Strait, was more nervous than Davey himself. With game time approaching, Ken came to give Davey some last-minute advice. Davey showed the pressure he felt to please his dad by the look on his face. I made an excuse to pull Davey away so I could settle him. I kept him close until the game started. Ken meant well, but he wasn't helping. With the game ready to start, Davey turned for the mound; Ken called to him one more time.

"Davey, wait! Just one more thing."

"What?!"

Davey snapped as he wheeled and faced his dad. This was a side of Davey I had never seen. The anxiety was too much; he was on the emotional edge. It was as though a curtain had been cast down from the heavens, separating Davey from his dad. Ken desperately wanted to rip the curtain down, but he didn't know how. He turned toward the dugout; I met him as he walked.

"Ken, we need to talk. Please don't be angry with me; I'm here to help. Giving any more advice right now is the worst thing to do. I know; I made this mistake with my older son. Right now you need to go sit down in the stands and not say a word. Let me take it from here."

I'd never confronted a father that way before. Ken's dad loved his son more than I possibly could. That was the basis I leaned upon in the hope he would understand.

"You're right. Thanks."

There was no sarcasm in his voice. He thanked me. *He thanked me.* Then he left for the bleachers and sat down.

We were waiting for Collin to put on the catcher's gear. I took the opportunity to settle Davey one more time.

"Davey, let's just play catch. Throw the ball to me right over the top." We didn't speak. We threw the ball back and forth. I increased the pace. Back and forth; back and forth. Faster, and with rhythm. Collin finished with the gear and was ready. The first batter came to the plate. Davey wound up and fired the ball.

"Strike one!"

The refrain became familiar.

"Strike two!"

"Strike three, you're out!"

Davey faced three batters. He threw nine pitches. *He threw nine strikes.* His dad grew more silent, and more pleased, with every pitch.

In search for our vision of eternity, why can't we remember? Can we knock down barriers, to our remembering? Ken stood behind the curtain. Davey ripped it back. Nine pitches, nine strikes, three outs. It was more than I ever hoped for. I stepped out of the dugout to meet Davey and congratulate him. I caught a brief glimpse of his eyes as he rushed by. They said everything. I would have been a fool to stop him. As I had hoped, Ken had shown his love for Davey by letting go. Davey then repaid his dad with unimaginable riches. He ran past me directly into the waiting arms of his father.

"Dad! Dad! Did you see that? I was great!"

So I remembered. All in flow; all in rhythm.

Chapter Seven—Speed

The Cubs came to bat in the bottom half of the first inning after Davey had retired the side, and things didn't go well. They did manage a run, but they should have scored more. The Dodgers had improved greatly over the course of the season. When they came to the plate, the Dodger hitters were always difficult to retire. They had also become a much better team defensively. Leading off for the Cubs, Buck reached first base with an infield single. Buck was a great leadoff hitter. He was fast, *the fastest of them all*. He showed his speed again by reaching second with a steal. Seth then drove a liner to center field, but the Dodger fielder made the catch. The ball would have fallen for a hit against any other team in the league, and I was frustrated. But I tried to not deviate from my focus. Buck needed to move to third base to improve his scoring chances. He raced to third on a passed ball by the catcher.

No question, Buck was fast. I had learned earlier in the season, unfortunately, that there are limits in the universe. There are negative consequences when natural law is not obeyed. In that instance, Buck was at first base. The hitter behind him ripped the ball to the outfield. Buck rounded second and headed for third. He was flying; the temptation to see him score was too great. I sent him for home. But it didn't matter how fast Buck ran. Not even Rickey Henderson, one of the greatest base runners ever in the major leagues, could have scored on that play. Buck was thrown out at the plate. As Buck walked toward the dugout, I caught up with him.

"I'm sorry, Buck. I shouldn't have sent you. It's just that you run so fast. I wanted to try."

"It's okay, Coach. I shouldn't have gone. It was my fault."

It wasn't his fault. I was the one who had tampered with the laws of the universe. Buck did not elect to run. I sent him from third to home with no chance for success. Buck's greatness included more than speed; he had great character. Even at twelve, Buck understood some of the burdens that all men eventually carry in the world. He took responsibility for *my* error. At that moment, he did the coaching.

———

Pete Henderson then came to the plate with Buck at third. Pete also hit a liner to center, and the fielder caught the fly for another out. Buck used his speed to tag up and score. I was disappointed, although not in Buck or Pete. The Cubs had already gotten two solid at-bats that should have netted more runs, but the Dodgers had turned those at-bats into outs.

The Cubs cleanup hitter, Justin Farmer, came to the plate next. It was terrific having Justin on the team. Justin had been overlooked as a baseball player to this point in his life. His large size and glasses perhaps gave the impression he was not an athlete. But after watching Justin play, I knew better. Justin was a tremendous athlete with huge untapped potential. There would be a point Justin would realize and capture his ability, and I quietly hoped to be there for that moment. Unfortunately, it was not this at-bat; Justin struck out. The inning was over, and the Cubs led, 1–0.

Davey struggled on the mound in the second inning. He retired the first hitter on a fly ball to center field, and then he walked the next two batters. Walks are the bane of solid defensive baseball. Good teams make pitchers pay for walks. Davey seemed to be pitching the ball well; he was just having trouble closing hitters out. There was another out on an infield grounder, and then the next hitter stroked a nice single up the middle that scored two runs. The Cubs paid for the walks. The two runs the Dodgers had scored were a direct result.

Davey then walked another. The last two hitters in the Dodgers' lineup had reached base. I was worried. I didn't want to switch pitchers too early, but a pitching change would be in order if Davey didn't find a way to quickly get one more out. The problem was complicated, for the Dodgers were at the top of their order, with their best hitters coming to the plate. Disaster loomed. Fortunately, the next batter grounded out to second base to end the inning. It could have been worse, but the score was 3–1, and the Cubs were trailing.

Sky led off in the bottom of the second inning. As he strode toward the plate, Sky paused and chatted with his teammates.

"I'm going to crush it," he predicted.

He continued and then stopped again and waved to his parents in the crowd.

"Hi, Mom!"

Sky wasn't really calling to his mom. He was performing for everyone. As he stepped into the batter's box, he discussed the game with the umpire.

"I'll let you know when it's a strike."

Sky talked to anyone who would listen. His chattiness hurt him. In the middle of conversation, the ball, the runner, and the game would pass him by. His ability for conversation, however, never bothered me. It was one of the things that made the game such a joy to be a part of. The game is a game for boys, to be played by boys. Sky was a twelve-year-old boy playing the game he loved. Unfortunately, late in the season Sky developed a bad attitude, not connected to his chattiness.

"Why do I always have to play second base? I don't want to play second base anymore. I want to play shortstop."

Sky's problems didn't end there.

"Did you see our shortstop? He missed the ball. What a loser! I'd be a way better shortstop. We need to change!"

Sky was just about finished.

"Did you see the umpire last game? He was terrible. He didn't have any idea what a strike was. If we have that umpire again, I'm going to show him what a strike really is."

Sky picked up his bat and shook it for emphasis. I wasn't sure what to do. I thought the world of Sky, and I couldn't get through. There seemed to be no alternative but to pull him aside. Sky was a meteor screaming toward the earth's atmosphere, and we were about to collide.

Chapter Eight—Tides

The universe operates within a framework of governing law. An example is the process of the moon's gravitational pull controlling the earth's ocean tides. Tidal control runs like clockwork. The ebbs and flows are so regular they are predicted and tabled. Although emotions of young boys are not nearly as predictable, they also operate successfully within a framework of law. No man has the ability to control the emotional tides that surge in a young boy; no man ought to try. But a man can, a man ought, to predict that emotion and ride its tide successfully to a safe port. The day is truly magical when a destructive tide is turned back.

Whether by the laws of equal and opposite reaction, force and acceleration, or gravity, the universe adheres to its laws absolutely. Law must also be invoked to govern in the worlds of boys. And although every boy is unique, that uniqueness exists within only a few differing frameworks. Some boys want to lead; some boys want to follow; other boys want to assert control. The key to riding a destructive tide to a safe port lies in applying the proper absolute—the how, what, and when of engagement—within the correct framework, according to the governing law.

———

I feel great anticipation at the beginning of each new season. The first few practices are critical to our new team's success. The boys gather on the field so that I can watch the new team. I'm not referring to watching baseball. Sure, the boys throw the ball, they catch the ball, and they hit the ball as we meet. I observe who can make the throw from third to first. I watch who can catch heat from the pitcher. I scrutinize who can throw that heat. But most importantly, I study the boys. I need to know each unique boy and his general framework to determine the future application of the absolutes.

The first practice of every new season concludes with *the talk*. Over the course of ten years, my son Tyler had become very familiar with *the talk*. He had jokingly coined that phrase. Though he tired of its repetition, he grew to understand its value. Boys need every activity to include a structure. Boys *want* every activity to include a structure. They won't tell you; that's part of being a boy. They will show you; they will press limits. Boys don't press because they are cruel and evil. They press because they want to know how far they can go. A wise teacher will invoke governing law before the pressing begins. Then he is in a position to apply the absolutes. I explained the governing law.

"Gentlemen, there are only three rules for our team. Keep these rules, and we will never have any problem. The first rule is that you never make fun of anyone on our team. Of course that means Blake, but it also means everyone else. Your fellow Cubs will become your best friends. Say hi when you see your teammates at school. Wave to your teammates as you notice them away from baseball. They will treat you well if you treat them well."

"The second rule has to do with baseball. Jerry Sloan, the coach of the Jazz, calls it 'playing forward.' I don't care if you make a mistake; I don't care if you miss the ball; I don't care if you strike out. I will never yell at you for making a mistake when you're playing your best. What you do after the mistake is far more important. If you hang your head, if you kick the dirt, if you throw your glove, if you yell at the umpire, *if you quit doing your best*, I will yell. You can't change outcome once a mistake is made. But you can make sure you don't make the same mistake again. Play hard. Play with your head up. Play forward."

"The third rule is very important. I am the only one allowed to talk to the umpire. Ever! I don't care if the umpire makes a bad call; I don't care if the umpire is unfair. His rule is law. If there ever is a big enough problem, I'll talk to him about it. I may even yell. But I am the only one on the team with that right."

With governing law in place, the team now depended absolutely on the absolutes.

———

Issues arise. Sky was caught in the pull of distant gravity; he was in danger of drifting into space. Correction was necessary. Someone needed to tow him back. I had learned to discipline individually, not collectively, to resolve problems. Sky and I had a one-on-one discussion.

"Sky, I told you before, I don't care if you miss the ball. I don't care if anyone misses the ball. I do care about what you do after you or anyone else misses the ball. If you whine or mope or complain, I won't put up with it. When I ask you to play a particular spot for the good of the team, you'd better do it. I'm tired of the griping; if it doesn't stop now, you will sit down even if we only have nine players. We'll take the out for being one player short rather than me listening to your whining. You'd better straighten up now."

Sky was much better after facing the absolute. His emotional tide had completed its ebb; now it was in its natural flow. I made sure I pulled Sky aside after the positive change and let him know I had seen the improvement. Hearing the return to banter from him was music; he had put his struggles behind and was ready to just play.

Boys with Down syndrome are no different than other boys when considering the absolutes. There are boys with Down syndrome who want to lead; there are boys with Down syndrome who want to follow; there are boys with Down syndrome who want to assert control. With *any* boy, one must first understand his uniqueness, within his framework. Governing law must be invoked. Then proper application of the absolutes can succeed.

———

Blake, the prince of emotional tides, was twelve when we went to that first Scout camp. He had a terrific experience. He roasted marshmallows by the fire. He swam in the lake. He rowed the boats. Most importantly, he slept in the tent. He loves sleeping in the tent. His favorite thing about the tent is making shadow puppets on the ceiling with the help of a flashlight. I always bring extra batteries.

Midweek was hike day at the camp. All the boys in camp had opportunity to hike into the Yellowstone wilderness. The boys in Blake's troop wanted to go to the tallest waterfall. I had been to that waterfall before, and I knew the twenty-mile hike was too much for Blake. There were obstacles along the way that he wouldn't be able to overcome. We were fortunate enough to find a smaller group, a group of about ten, who were hiking to a closer waterfall. I thought Blake was capable, but I had hidden away the absolutes, tucked them away into the deepest recesses of the universe, ready for retrieval in the event of an emergency.

Terraced Falls was wonderful. Blake was terrific. We reached the falls at noon and enjoyed a pleasant lunch in the sun. There was a rock outcropping that allowed a spectacular view of the cascade. After lunch, each boy took his turn approaching the waterfall. Unfortunately, there are no railings in the wilderness. The boys stood on the edge of a fifty-foot cliff for the view. That danger, in and of itself, was enough to keep Blake from the falls. The problem was compounded by loose shale near the edge. The poor footing, combined with Blake's lack of fear, spelled disaster.

In the world of his abilities, I have never treated Blake any differently than any of the other boys. I have never intentionally placed limits on his activity. I have always tried to allow him to determine those limits. There are, however, exceptions. It was unwise, and unsafe, to allow him near the waterfall. But Blake wanted to assert control. I could read by his eyes that he wanted to approach the edge as all the other boys had. When I told him no, he didn't understand. He became belligerent. It was time to retrieve the absolute.

"Blake, did you know there's a store back at camp?" I had kept this knowledge hidden from him since the moment we arrived. I didn't know when the time would come to reveal the secret, but I knew the time *would* come.

Blake's attention was momentarily diverted from the waterfall.

"Really?"

"Yes. It has Butterfingers, Reese's, and chips. It has root beer too. Let's gather up our lunch and start back for camp. When we get back, the store will be open. But we don't have time to look at the waterfall. We'd better start back now."

Was it simple bribery? Maybe. But what begins as bribery in youth transitions to sacrifice in maturity. Time and effort are required to see the principles penetrate, but with persistence the wisdom does come. Sacrifice means giving up something good for something better. By applying the absolutes, the engagement, within Blake's framework, the danger of the cliff was replaced with safety and a Butterfinger. As boys grow, Butterfingers must be replaced with abstract but far more important rewards, such as respect, integrity, and honor. But in that moment, it was a Butterfinger that moved Blake forward.

———

Sky started the bottom half of the second inning with a double. The team had high hopes for a big inning. Unfortunately, first Collin and then Johnny Coates struck out. Blake then came to bat. It was his initial plate appearance on that magical night. He stood tall in his freshly pressed Cubs uniform as he readied for the first pitch.

"Strike one!"

Blake's beauty lies in his simplicity. When it comes to conversation, he is the antithesis of Sky. Blake looked eye-to-eye with the umpire.

"NO!"

That was it. There was nothing else. No "that wasn't a strike," no "that was a terrible call," not even "c'mon, ump, give me a break." Just "NO!" Clearly and simply stated.

"Blake, settle down."

"But, Dad, he say 'strike'!"

"That's because it was a strike. Now swing at the pitch, and hit the ball!"

From time to time, boys show great skill when dealing with tidal emotions. Blake was still angry, and he turned to the umpire. "You don't say strike anymore!" he demanded.

The boy behind the mask was only a year or two older than Blake. Yet he stilled the surge. He was calm and encouraging as he spoke.

"I have to call it a strike when it's over the plate. You swing the bat hard now and try to hit the ball." The next pitch came.

"Strike two!"

The umpire's voice echoed through the park as Blake swung the bat. Blake's swing was so hard, it carried Blake into a pirouette. Unfortunately, he did not make contact with the ball. He stepped out of the batter's box and discussed the issue with his bat.

"You hit the ball right here!" he ordered as he held the spot on the barrel where he hoped to will contact. He stepped back into the box and waited for the next pitch.

"Strike three, you're out!"

Cosmic catastrophe! Blake stomped toward the Cubs dugout. He ripped the batting helmet from his head. It looked as if he were planning to throw it. I met him in an attempt to reverse the tide.

"Blake, it was the third strike. You have to go sit down."

"But, Dad," Blake protested, "he say I'm out!"

"You are out, Blake. The pitcher threw three strikes. Let's go back to the dugout."

"But, Dad," he pleaded, "please…just one more!"

There is nothing in any universe more difficult than telling Blake no. But I love him.

"No. Let's go sit down."

"I not going!"

He broke free and angrily ran down the third baseline. I smiled and laughed. I remembered a similar incident with Blake when he was walked by a pitcher. He refused to go to first base. Just as this strikeout, that walk had nothing to do with anger at the umpire; he only wanted to hit the baseball.

———

Blake thinks linearly. He moves from A to B to C to D. Though he does not process quickly, his thinking is in perfect flow, in perfect rhythm. I didn't understand his process until he explained it to me. It was after he turned twelve and had been ordained a deacon. He had worked through the details of passing the sacrament and enjoyed success. His participation added reverence and respect to the ceremony. Sunday morning came, and we were running late. I moved Blake quickly through his morning process. I began by waking him. Blake's step A began with the quilt. He pulled the blanket over his head, thinking that the darkness had made him disappear. Under the covers, he existed in a solitary world, free to live according to his own desire. I waited the predetermined amount of time, and then I pulled the blanket back.

"Are you ready for church, Blakey?"

He rolled over and looked at me. His look signaled we were now moving to step B. "I'll go get your clothes. Don't go back to sleep." I brought his clothes to him, and he started to dress. He struggled with buttons, so I tried to speed the process by doing a few. My first mistake. The worst thing to do with Blake when you want to hurry the process is to let him know you're trying to hurry the process.

"No, Dad! Don't help me."

He finished on his own. The clock was ticking, and we still had to move to step C, breakfast, and step D, brushing his teeth and combing his hair. I plotted that we could do breakfast in the car. It was my second, and largest, mistake. I'd already set him off by helping with the buttons. Changing anything else in the process would lead to disaster. As Blake came down the stairs, I told him I had some toast and juice ready; he could eat on the way.

"No, Dad, I don't want to. I eat right *here.*" He pointed to his place at the table.

"Blake, we can still be on time to pass the sacrament if we leave right now. Brush your teeth, and let's go." I pushed him to the bathroom. He grudgingly complied. By not allowing him to sit in his usual spot at the table, I sensed his axis had been tilted too far, but I pressed on. He ate the toast and drank the juice as we drove to church. As he ate, I mistakenly believed I had successfully changed the step. Blake regularly sat at the table to eat; now he was eating in the car. I was proud of myself. I had conquered the process.

Blake, however, was not persuaded. He sat quietly with the other boys until it was time for the sacrament. He rose with the boys to receive his tray. As the priest at the table leaned to hand Blake the dish, the riptide hit the beach.

"No! I won't do it!"

He turned and stormed down the aisle. The eighteen-year-old priest was left dumbfounded. He tried desperately to imagine what he could have done to provoke the response. He hadn't done anything. Blake was mad at me. Blake does not, Blake cannot, suppress his emotions. The surge pressed forward. He had been forced to change the routine of breakfast, and this was the consequence. Because Blake was new to the ceremony, I had positioned myself close. I met him halfway down the aisle, and we hurried outside. His emotions continued to rush forward. The surge subsided when he had worked though his feelings. We don't change steps anymore. Blake must be allowed to process.

———

So I stood still; I did not pursue as Blake took several steps down the third baseline. He turned back and looked at me. I was silent as I opened my arms to him. When the time was right, I spoke.

"It's all right, Blake. You'll have another chance. Let's go sit down and get ready for your next turn."

Blake slowly came to me. I put my arm around him and loosely held him.

"Okay, Dad," he said as he put his head on my shoulder. "But you tell him not to say 'out' anymore!"

"I'll tell him."

I grinned to the umpire as we passed. He looked back and smiled with maturity beyond his years. The inning was over, and absolutes, the rules of engagement in the universe, had turned back the tide.

Chapter Nine—Needs

The top of the third inning went much better for Davey. He retired the side, and the score remained 3–1. The Cubs were trailing and coming to bat. Tony Jacobson led off. He was a good hitter; he was also a boy with autism.

It bothered me when Tony was placed on the Cubs, although the issue had nothing to do with Tony. I love Blakey; I coach for Blakey. Because of Blake's having Down syndrome, the league had a tendency to make the team I coached the discard. Problems other coaches didn't want to deal with were given to me because of my experience with Blake's disability. I felt complimented to be trusted with difficult issues, but I also felt leaned upon. The issue was one of giving one coach, of giving one team, more opportunity than it could handle. My sensitivity wasn't without precedent.

————

At the beginning of every season, the league put together team rosters and forwarded the lists to their respective coaches. Receiving the list always preceded making *the phone call*. I dreaded making that phone call. Blake didn't progress at the same rate as other boys because of Down syndrome. That precluded us from picking an age group for Blake to stay with season after season. Every year brought a new group of players and parents and a new set of challenges—hence, the dreaded phone call. I had no more experience coaching children with disabilities than any other parent in the league. Blake was the first boy with Down syndrome I'd ever been near for any length of time, and he was the only boy with Down syndrome I knew playing baseball. It was as much an experiment for me as it was for anyone else. Armed with the names and phone numbers of the new team in hand, every season I set about calling each parent to welcome his son.

Parents have great aspirations for their boys. Parents want their sons to be members of the best team. Parents want each season's experience to be a springboard to bigger things. I understood those dreams. I had an older son without disability. Because of those hopes, there were times that parents couldn't see past Blake's having Down syndrome, and they overlooked the advantages to being on Blake's team. For example, Blake did not play at anyone else's expense. He didn't do much more than stand when he was in the field; thus, the league allowed me to play nine players in addition to him. I also had no illusions about Blake's ability. He wasn't going to pitch; he wasn't going to catch; he wasn't going to play shortstop. My dream for Blake was simpler. I wanted just to see him play.

Although I wasn't completely sure how to explain the advantages, most of the time the ice-breaking phone call was positive. Even though the call was generally well received, there was a call before Blake's second season in the Mustang Division that didn't go well.

"Hi, are you Billy's dad?

"Yes, I am."

"This is Jeff Curtis. I'm Billy's new coach, and I'm calling to welcome him to our team. We're glad to have him with us, and we're going to have a great season. I'll go over the schedule for the season with you in a minute; first, I need to explain the team's makeup. My son Blake is one of the players."

"Yes?"

Most parents weren't alarmed by a father–son combination. Every team generally has that component. It was the bombshell afterward that was the surprise.

"Blake is twelve. He has Down syndrome, and he *will play*."

I'm not sure I handled the *will play* part well. I was scarred from the *counting* experience in the Pinto Division. I wanted to clearly establish with every parent that Blake would play, and there was to be no further discussion. We broached the subject once; then it was done. Billy's dad apparently didn't see advantage to Billy playing baseball in Blake's universe.

"He has Down syndrome? He's going to play?"

"Yes."

The rest of the phone call was awkward. We quickly went through the details of the schedule and finished. To his credit, Billy's father called me directly about his concerns. To his fault, he lied about them.

"Billy is playing on too many teams this season. We just don't have time to be to every practice and every game. We really are sorry, but Billy won't be playing on your team."

There was a pause.

"Oh, and your boy with Down syndrome playing? Good luck with *that*."

I'm not completely sure where in the world *that* came from. It made me wonder if I were right to be there just for Blakey. In *Star Trek III: The Search for Spock*, Captain Spock and Jim Kirk talked:

> Captain Spock: My father says that you have been my friend. You came back for me.
>
> Kirk: You would have done the same for me.
>
> Captain Spock: Why would you do this?

Kirk: Because the needs of the one…outweigh the needs of the many.

Captain Spock: [pacing] I have been and ever shall be your friend.[5]

I don't know if the needs of the one outweigh the needs of the many. I don't know if it is just. I do know saving Spock saved the world countless times. I'm seeking to understand the laws of the universe. I hope there is a time that Blake looks at me and says, "I have been and ever shall be your friend." But there are twelve boys on a baseball team. I needed to address the needs of the other eleven too. In fairness to Billy's father, he said what he thought about *that*. I drew my own conclusions based upon my life in Blake's universe. But the call was instructive. Coaching Blake's team had to become more than being about Blake. Every boy that shared Blake's team needed to have a worthwhile experience. I committed to become the best I could for all the boys. Baseball is easy to quantify. Batting average, RBIs, ERA, on-base percentage, slugging percentage—these are all baseball quantifiers that measure success. I focused on every one of those measures to help each boy. Most importantly, I have sought to focus on the unquantifiable; I focus on each boy.

Tony deserved just as much opportunity to play as Blake. I loved Tony. I put my feelings of being used aside. I worked to make sure the season was a good experience for Tony and for every boy on the team. I sought the universal view. The course to follow was clear; I took what the league had given and made the best of it. Tony earned his place.

———

Tony stepped quietly to the plate. He pulled his batting helmet close to his eyes. Tony's autism was mild and, at least from a

———

5   "The Needs of the One," *Star Trek III: The Search for Spock*, directed by
    Leonard Nimoy (Los Angeles: Paramount Pictures, 1984), DVD.

distance, unrecognizable. It was clear, however, that Tony did have struggles. That made his playing with the Cubs all the more satisfying and meaningful as the Cubs continued to win.

"Ball four!" the umpire shouted. Tony began the inning with a walk. It was great to have a base runner, but the season had not been kind to either Tony or Blakey when they were on the base paths. Both had been doubled-out multiple times because they didn't understand how to tag up, or they didn't realize the pitcher could pick them off base. How do you explain tagging up to someone with autism, to someone with Down syndrome? How do you explain leading off? How do you explain stealing a base? There is no manual. But as surely as the moon is held in its orbit by the earth, as surely as ocean tides ebb and flow, every boy, *every boy*, can learn.

———

Tony had been doubled-up in the first game of the tournament. As he stood at first base, I vividly remembered the earlier play.

"Get back to the base!" I screamed to Tony as the fielder caught the ball and readied his throw to make the second out. Unfortunately, it was too late. I hadn't yelled in anger. Spurred by competiveness, I yelled to win the game. I felt terrible. I knew I had violated the absolutes. I had not approached Tony within his framework. Then I compounded the problem. I ran on the field after the out to make sure he was okay; I wanted to make sure he knew I wasn't angry.

"Tony, come here and let's talk. Tony!"

I pleaded as he ran away in fear. I then dropped my attempt to talk with Tony as I drop my razor in the morning when I clip my lip. It seemed there was no need to continue, making the cut deeper. All that could be done was to place tissue on the wound and hope to stop the bleeding.

Later, I took a moment to call Tony's parents and explain the incident. Chris Jacobson, Tony's father, was really good about the entire episode.

"Tony is fine," Chris had said, with little emotion. "I didn't even know anything had happened."

I also went to Tony, and he had forgotten the entire incident. I was grateful. I made a mental note to make sure that I never made that mistake again. There was peace in my universe, the balance maintained by the absolute. In a later game against the Rays, Tony led off first base. He momentarily lost concentration, and the Rays' pitcher noticed. He made his move to first while Tony was unaware. Tony was picked off and called out. It didn't matter to me. I too had learned the absolutes. Tony was getting better.

And what of Blake? He could hit the ball, but could he steal a base? Throughout the course of the season, I tried every way possible to teach him how to steal. I even tried using him as a decoy. In an earlier game, Blake had been on first, and the Cubs had a runner on third. We needed a run, and Blake was the bait. I tried and tried to get Blake to run to second to coerce a throw from the catcher. That would allow the base runner on third to steal home. Blake wouldn't leave the base. He was convinced he had to stay.

Later while we were still playing, even though the outcome of the game had been decided, the opposing coach came to me. Blake was at first base again. The coach had watched us try coaxing Blake to steal. He also wanted to see Blake learn the game.

"Send him to second. I'll make sure my catcher doesn't throw the ball."

It was a wonderful gesture on his part. It gave me opportunity to teach Blake. I begged and begged Blake to run but to no avail. The pitcher threw two pitches, and each time Blake refused to leave the base. I was exasperated. I called time and asked for one more favor.

"Coach, will you let me run with him?"

Blake and I stood together at first base as I formulated a plan.

"Blake, let's race. When the ball crosses the plate, you say go. Then we'll race to second base."

Blake's eyes brightened. He smiled in agreement. The pitch crossed the plate, and he shouted, "Go!" Many who were watching laughed at the sight of us: a bald, overweight, forty-something man and his son with Down syndrome racing for second. But if baseball is art, the race was poetry. We made it safely.

"You did it, Blake! You stole the base!" Blake was happy. He understood. Ken Strait, Davey's dad, often coached first base for the Cubs. After that initial success, and under his watchful eye, Blake would run for second on a passed ball. Blake stole three bases on his own. His pleasure playing baseball had now grown.

———

I smiled at those successes as I mentally returned. Tony took a small lead off first base. The pitcher noticed and made his move to the bag. Fortunately, Tony was focused. The earlier emotional crest had been ridden to a safe port, according to the absolutes. He stepped safely back to the base. The pitcher, however, made an errant throw. On that day Chris Jacobson was coaching first, and he sent Tony safely to second for the steal. The mockingbirds had learned and grown. Tidal emotions were in flow, and the earth moved forward in its rotation. The vision opened to my mind the possibility that, though the Cubs were still behind when the error occurred, they would win the game. Perhaps it was my turn to briefly see the broader view.

All in flow; all in rhythm.

The rest of the inning was okay, not great. Davey hit a grounder to the infield that advanced Tony to third, and then Tony scored on a base hit by Buck. That made the score 3–2 as the inning came to a close.

Chapter Ten—Negotiation

Although I sensed victory, events in the fourth inning didn't bear out the premonition. Seth was ready to pitch, as Davey had never pitched more than two consecutive innings and now had pitched three. Davey had pitched well; he did much better than I thought he would. The game was moving quickly. It seemed we might play the full six innings within the time limit. The Cubs needed one inning from Seth, but he struggled, struggled so much that I wondered if he could finish. It wasn't that he couldn't throw strikes. He was having a hard time closing hitters out. Unfortunately, each at-bat always came down to just one pitch, and this had been the hitters' day. Then the rhythm drill kicked in; Seth looked better and threw hard. He finished, but he gave up five runs in the process. On the positive, he struck out the Dodgers' number three and four hitters to close out the inning.

Seth was the bridge between Davey and the Cubs' ace, Pete Henderson. By the time Seth was through, it looked as if it might not matter. A six-run deficit (the score was now 8–2) was much to overcome. Still, I felt the rhythm. I remembered the play that triggered Tony to score; I was confident of the team's success.

The bottom of the fourth inning went well. Justin hit the ball hard, Sky followed with a hit, and Collin walked to get on base. With Collin on first base and Johnny Coates at the plate, the best strategy was to move Collin to scoring position. When the first pitch of Johnny's at-bat reached the catcher, the catcher let the ball get by. Collin had read the passed-ball steal sign, but he hesitated before leaving for second. He was a great boy, and I loved him. He had been terrific with Blakey, laughing and playing with him at every game. From time to time, he even sought Blake out. Unfortunately, Collin ran slowly. He was about the slowest player I've ever coached. He understood the game; he just didn't run very fast. As Collin pondered the steal, the catcher tracked down the ball and threw to second. The ball arrived well before Collin, but the throw got past the second baseman. Collin was lucky to have made it safely, and he was now in a position to score. The next pitch reached the catcher, and the ball got by again. Collin did not have the green light to steal, but he took it upon himself to run a second time.

Men have gazed at the universe through a telescope for hundreds of years. They have seen light from stars, light that has traveled millions of miles and eons of time. The light may have been the reflection of a newly created planet; it may have been the mirrored image of a star's destruction; ultimately, it is a view from the past. In the next instant, Collin was running again, but the distance from second to third seemed to have increased exponentially, and Collin's speed was similar to light from the past. Collin ran to third base in slow motion. It was déjà vu, like we were watching him steal second base all over again, only this time it was a much easier throw for the catcher.

"Don't come, Collin!" I screamed. "*No!*"

It was all for naught. Collin was on his way. The throw to third was in time, but high. Collin slid under the tag. A wide grin spread across his face. His smile was contagious. I laughed out loud with him.

"Collin, you scare me to death," I said as I removed my hat and wiped the perspiration from my brow. I noted the perfuming effect of the shampoo on my balding head was wearing off. Twice Collin had barely been safe; both times he should have been out.

All in flow; all in rhythm.

Johnny Coates then hit a shot to center field. It was a terrific hit, but the same center fielder made another great catch. Collin was able to tag up and cross home plate, making the score 8–5, as both Justin and Sky had scored earlier. Then Blake came to bat.

As he walked to the plate, he flashed several hand signals to the umpire. I couldn't figure out what he was doing. Had he sneaked away between innings and joined a gang? After he finished the signals, he spoke to the ump.

"You don't call strike anymore!"

I said before that my emotions are similar to the big bang. So are Blake's. But his differ in that after the initial explosion, he immediately moves to creation's refinement. He doesn't hold a grudge. He does not dwell on hurt or anger. But that doesn't mean he isn't willing to negotiate. It occurred to me what the hand signals were. Blake was mimicking the umpire, showing the pitch count. He wanted no strikes called. Unfortunately, Blake was in his universe, and the umpire was not. Blake struck out.

Tony then found his way to first base but was left standing on the bag as Davey struck out to end the inning. The Cubs had scored three runs to inch closer to the Dodgers. As the team ran out to the field, Blake stayed in the dugout. He was cross. I felt another negotiation coming. It's all about negotiation with Blake.

"Grab your mitt, Blakey. It's time to go to right field."

"I not going!"

"Come on, Blake. We need you in the field. Do you want me to go with you?"

"No. You stay *right* here."

"Why don't you want to play?"

"He say I'm out!"

Blake had made progress in the field, and I loved watching him play. When he began, he wouldn't stand for more than one batter. He spent most of his time chasing butterflies and picking dandelions. Over time, his attention span and his understanding increased. He achieved a major milestone when he stood for an entire inning. Next, we worked on playing catch. I love to play catch. To this day, I love to go outside and throw the ball with anyone. It was difficult with Blake. There seemed to be no possibility we would ever be able to stand together and just throw the ball. But he got better. Just as Willie Mays, he learned the basket catch. It wasn't on Willie's level, but it worked. Although the basket catch was improvement, I didn't think I would ever get Blake to lift his glove. He seemed destined to always catch with his glove extended straight out and the ball aimed into his mitt. Then Blake crossed into Chase Everett's orbit.

Chase plays on every team. Chase is in every Scout troop. Chase is in every class at school. His name isn't always Chase; it may be Jay or Dane or Cameron. But there is a Chase in every group. Chase is the boy all the others want to be. He is generally tall, handsome, and outgoing. Sometimes he isn't very kind, but this Chase was. He took time for Blake, and the other boys aligned.

———

There was no angle to the shadows cast from the midsummer sun. It was directly overhead for the afternoon practice. The team was warming up, and Blake was playing catch with me.

He stopped.

Chase was catching and throwing the ball nearby. Blake watched intently as Chase raised his glove to catch the ball and dropped his glove to throw. The rhythmic motion was mesmerizing. Catch the ball, make the throw, drop the glove; catch the ball, make the throw, drop the glove. I'd seen Blake act this way before. I wasn't sure what he was watching, but for a long time I didn't interrupt.

"Are you ready for the ball, Blake?"

Blake looked up and smiled. His mouth did not move; the gleam was in his eyes. Rather than holding his glove out in front for a basket catch, he held his glove up, imitating Chase. There was a danger. Learning to catch hadn't been easy; my aim wasn't the best. I had hit Blake before. We worked through the pain of bad throws, but with his glove held high, if he missed the ball, it would hit him in his face instead of his arm or his chest.

"Are you sure you want me to throw it there?"

"Throw it right *here*," he said as he pointed to the glove's pocket.

I let go of the ball with trepidation. The throw was true. It found the glove's heart. Blake smiled broadly. It was not the smile of pride; it was the smile of accomplishment. The basket-catch days were over. Chase taught Blake to catch without ever throwing him the ball.

———

The negotiation for right field continued. Blake's negotiating skills had been finely tuned. In the beginning, he negotiated for chips. He moved up to root beer. His skills reached their apex when he demanded an entire meal. He honed his skills at the barbershop. Although they weren't in the beginning, haircuts had become a huge wrestle. It may have been the scissors; it may have been the clipper's buzz. Whatever it was, Blake would go crazy when he went for a trim. I tried everything. I tried to read to him. I tried to sing to him (now *that* was scary). I even took the TV/VCR combo to the salon to watch a movie with him. Nothing worked. I was beaten down and tired. Searching for resolution, I let go of every emotion I felt, excepting my love for Blake. With that love in my heart, I went to him. I tried to reason with him. Well, as reason is defined in Blake's universe.

"Blake, I can't do this anymore. What can we do to make it easier?"

"I don't know, Dad."

"How about a bag of chips? Will you be good if I get you a bag of chips when we're done?"

"Yeah. Chips."

Blake was true to his word. Chips worked well for a while. Then the dynamics of the universe changed.

"Remember, we'll get a bag of chips after the haircut if you're good."

"No."

I was taken aback. Chips had been a staple; chips always worked. I didn't know what to do.

"What do you mean no? Don't you want a bag of chips?"

"No," he sighed as he slowly shook his head, "no chips."

I panicked. "Are you sure you don't want chips? We'll get a big bag of Cheetos."

He waited, adding to the drama. Then he finally answered. "No," he drawled, "no chips. Chicken and French fries!"

Since that escalation, our relationship had evolved. My application of the absolutes had improved, surpassed only by the growth of Blake's maturity. There would be no chicken and French fries on that magical night.

"Blake, do you want your next turn at bat?" He could tell by my tone I was irritated. His answer was long and drawn out; he finished with the hint of question.

- 76 -

"Yeeessss?" Then he paused. "Dad, you mad at me?"

"No. I'm not mad. Go out to the field."

"Oh, all right!" He stormed from the dugout to right field.

Pete Henderson took the ball in the top of the fifth inning, and he did what he does; he mowed the Dodgers down. He struck out the first two batters he faced. The number three hitter walked and moved around the bases to third, but Pete left him stranded by striking out the next batter.

The Cubs were still behind 8–5, with the top of their batting order coming to the plate. Buck and Seth both hit singles to start the inning. Pete Henderson hit a triple to drive them in. With no outs, the score was 8–7. Justin came to the plate with Pete at third and struck out. The lines of Justin's potential and performance had still not crossed. Sky hit a single to score Pete Henderson. Collin and Johnny Coates then both struck out; the score was 8–8 at the end of five innings.

Pete faced the minimum number of batters in the sixth: three up and three down. The Cubs had Blake, Tony, and Davey at the plate in the bottom of the inning, and unfortunately all three struck out. The game ended in a tie as time expired. One more inning would be played, deciding who would face the Rays for first place. There was no need for concern. The Cubs had the last at-bat with the top of the batting order coming to the plate. The Dodgers did manage to string together two hits to take the lead in their half of the inning, 9–8. It didn't matter. Buck led off the bottom half of the inning with a hit, and Seth followed with another. With base runners on second and third, Pete doubled to end the game. The final score was 10–9.

I smiled as the team left the field. I was happy for the boys, and I was happy for Blake. Blake had never won a baseball trophy; now he had one guaranteed. He came to me regularly and asked if the Cubs would win. Trophies were awarded to both the first-place team and the second-place team in the tournament. The win over the Dodgers ensured the Cubs no less than second place. As difficult as it was to pull away from that satisfaction, however, I brought myself back. I gathered the team near the dugout for a brief discussion.

"Gentlemen, we need to be gracious to the Dodgers. We need to congratulate them for a well-played game."

I loved circling the team to yell. We came together at the beginning of each game to yell, again before batting in our half of each inning to yell, and we came together at the conclusion of each game to yell. Most coaches circle their boys and have each put one hand in the center to begin. I do too, with one exception. I hate the count. I despise the "one, two, three" that every team repeats before they cheer. The "one, two, three" disrupts the rhythm. The counting detracts from the focus. I prefer knowing I have everyone's attention. Rather than counting, we begin the process with my hand lifting. The yell begins at the drop of my hand. The boys learned this approach at the beginning of every season. The Cubs struggled, not always paying attention and not always doing their best—but not this day.

I put out my hand while the team circled round. Tony stood near with his hat pulled closely to his eyes. Sky, for the first time, was silent and focused. Davey stood hatless, his red hair screaming, "I did it!" to the universe. Johnny Coates smiled with pleasure as he considered his contribution. I thought I saw the light of Rickey Henderson's reflection as I glanced at Collin. Seth stood by Blake with his hat turned sideways. Blake was just Blake.

The remainder of the team followed, each placing a hand on top of mine. Not a word was spoken, even as to what we would yell. The team stood together as one in their circular world. I lifted my hand, and the cheer began. It was loud, resolute, and in complete unison.

"Good game, Dodgers!"

The Cubs shouted together and with great joy; the circle then broke as each team member ran to home plate to shake hands with the Dodgers.

It was all in flow; all in rhythm.

Chapter Eleven—Contradiction

There are moments in the life of a boy when time stands still. There are moments in the life of a boy when he becomes the center of the universe, when the gravitational pull of the moment is drawn to him as powerfully as the earth's orbit is pulled by the sun. There are moments in the life of a boy that are never to be forgotten; they live on through his memories and through to his children.

These moments are indelibly imprinted upon a boy's soul. However, as the boy's mortality spins toward manhood, these moments turn inward, pushed back in memory, becoming hidden from view. It is as if the moments have rotated into the shadows rather than remaining in the sun's full light. The boy wants desperately to hold these moments, to stop the earth's rotation, or at least slow it so that the moments remain in the light of day. He memorizes the moments; he burns their sounds, their smells, and their sights into his mind. He photographs the moments; he writes them down; he tells them to anyone who will listen.

Fortunately, these moments never disappear. Carved upon the stone tablet of time, they wait for the trigger that will swing them again to the light; they wait for the sound, the smell, or the sight that will cast them again into the radiance; they wait for the flash that will illuminate them again in the brightness, making them again as real as they were when they happened. In the continuum of never-ending time, the marker representing the two-hour baseball game the Cubs had just finished was such a moment. I had traveled through a galaxy of moments just as the one just witnessed, and I understood its importance. What I did not understand was we had only reached the meridian; the travel of the earth on its axis had only moved far enough to complete a half-rotation. It was noon. The revolution's completion would be far more memorable, a glorious sunset. The championship game the Cubs had earned the right to play would be unforgettable.

I tried to direct my thoughts to getting the team ready for the second game. It was difficult. I was thrilled the team had come back to win, and I wanted to savor. I couldn't help but think of Todd and Kathy. Blake's team had played Todd's son's team two seasons after *we* had tried to artificially determine Blake's value in the world. Blake had singled that game, scoring two, pushing the game-winning run across the plate. Though *we* lost that game, *we* won the championship that season. *We* got what *we* wanted. I did too. I was the fortunate one; I was with Blake. I thought of Billy's dad and the Billy I never knew, the Billy who never got to play ball with Blake. From one world's view, Billy had been denied a great opportunity. Billy could easily have been Chase Everett. He could have been the boy who taught Blake to catch. I'm sure Billy is a great baseball player, and I hope he is a friend. I thought of the man with the secret. I considered his anger, slamming the dugout pole with a bat, angry with Blake's success. I still don't understand. Blake had offered; the man refused. I hoped he would one day meet another physician that could successfully perform the cataract surgery he so desperately needed.

It had been a great season. The team was now guaranteed a trophy and no less than second place in the Bronco Division tournament. The boys, however, had other ideas. They were preparing for the Rays on their own. They had not lost focus. They were looking forward to playing again. They had achieved a portion of their own dream. They were playing for the championship. They wanted to win.

Ted, the Rays' coach and the all-star coach, had been watching intently and came to congratulate the Cubs.

"Great game, Coach. Take as much time as you need to get ready, and then let me know, and we'll start."

"Thanks, Ted. Give us a few minutes to recover, and then we'll be ready."

I laughed to myself. I wasn't quite sure how Ted could control game time. He wasn't a league official; he was coaching just as I was. I put him out of my mind. There would be nothing that would spoil the elation I felt from the win over the Dodgers. I left Ted and went to check on my team.

"Gentlemen, take a minute to rest. Make sure you get some water. Then we'll get ready to play."

As the team rested and talked among themselves, I set about laying out the pitcher–catcher battery for the championship game. The league rules allowed for the boys to pitch seven innings in one day, regardless of how many games that might entail. The rules also required that if a pitcher pitched a single pitch into a fourth inning, he had to rest forty hours before he could pitch again. Pete Henderson, the Cubs' ace, had pitched three innings, Davey had pitched three innings, and Seth, one.

The Rays had come through the double-elimination tournament winner's bracket. They had not lost. The Cubs had worked their way to the upcoming game through the one-loss bracket. If the Cubs lost, the tournament was over; if the Cubs won, there would be a one-game, winner-take-all playoff between the same two teams. It would have been foolish to save any pitching for the next day. I reasoned we had to win the first game in order to play the second. I planned on throwing Pete Henderson as much as possible. Unfortunately, Pete had only four more innings he could pitch; I had to get at least one inning out of someone else. I was leery about starting Seth. It was important for Seth to succeed, and he seemed to function better pitching in relief. He still had the possibility of six full innings of pitching later in the game; I decided to start Davey again.

The Cubs were ready to go. Game time was 8:11 PM. The Cubs were at bat. Buck led off the game and struck out. Seth and Pete both followed with infield outs. I wasn't surprised that the Cubs started flat; after all, they had just won an emotional contest that had gone into extra innings. At that point, all I was hoping for was a good game from the team. I settled in for the bottom of the inning.

Davey didn't pitch badly. He did give up four runs, but he was throwing the ball well and throwing in the strike zone. His accuracy was his biggest enemy. The pitches were right over the plate, and the Rays were locking down on them. After the third straight hit and the cleanup hitter coming to the plate, I called time-out. I walked to the mound to talk with Davey. I had no intention of taking him out of the game, but I needed to find a way to help him reclaim the inside of the plate. I planned the conversation as I walked. Seth was catching, and he stood up to follow. I motioned him to stay back. Only Davey needed to listen. The team hadn't always had the utmost confidence in him, and I didn't want to compound the problem.

"Davey, you're pitching well and throwing strikes. The problem is the Rays are zeroing in on your pitches. You need to hit the next batter."

Davey was astonished! I could see the conflict that had arisen in his mind. I hadn't calculated his reaction, and I should have. This was, after all, Farmington, *Utah*. Most of the boys from Farmington had been trained by their parents against aggression. They never considered hitting a batter with a pitch on purpose.

"Davey, sometimes hitting a batter in a game is part of baseball. You *never, ever* throw at someone's head, but sometimes you have to hit a guy in the back to make the other team think you're wild. That moves the hitter away and gives you back the inside of the plate."

Davey swallowed hard. It was as close as he came to speaking. I wondered for a moment if Davey could muster the flame inside to match that burning red hair. "Don't worry about it, Davey. You'll be okay. If there's a problem after you hit him, I'll be right here. You can do it."

I left Davey to his own thoughts and hurried back to the dugout. He stepped to the mound and looked nervously toward me. Then he nodded his head in agreement. It was against his judgment, but he would do it. He wound up and fired the ball. The pitch went behind the batter and into the dirt. I laughed to myself. It was a nervous laugh but not without humor. I had asked Davey to do something that he wasn't capable of, and I felt bad for it. The hue of Davey's hair and his personality were contradictory; rather, Davey's smile projected the gentleness and graciousness of his demeanor.

The pitch, nevertheless, had the desired effect. The cleanup hitter for the Rays was confused. He was worried Davey was wild. The plan worked well enough to help Davey strike him out. The Rays got another hit before the inning was over, but Davey had regained confidence. He ended the inning with two more successive strikeouts. Unfortunately, the damage was severe; the Rays took the early lead, 4–0.

The top half of the second inning was much better. Justin led off for the Cubs with a hit. He was beginning to hit his stride even though I had made it more difficult. It was an odd twist. He had, in a way, been punished for making the all-star team. His natural swing was from the outside to the inside; he consistently brought the knob of the bat from the outside of the swing to the inside and then in front of his body. It was very effective when hitting an inside pitch, but it was inefficient when hitting the ball out over the plate. I had explained this to Ted at the all-star tryouts to help him prepare Justin for the all-star season. I had revealed the secret of how to pitch to Justin in league play. My intentions were good; I wanted to help Justin succeed as an all-star. Unfortunately, after the revelation, he seldom saw an inside pitch against the Rays. It was quite satisfying to see him muster a hit.

Sky followed Justin with a walk, Collin hit a single, and Johnny Coates another. The Cubs were gaining momentum, trimming the deficit. Blake then came to the plate for his first at-bat in the championship game. It was a moment in time a father dreams of, a moment in time when everything stands still, a moment when outcome is irrelevant.

Blake was in full ritual mode at the plate. He began with holding up his right hand behind him, signaling timeout to the umpire. He continued by knocking the dirt out of his spikes with his bat. Then he then dug his cleats into the dirt as he prepared for the ball. Last, he pointed the bat to the fence he planned on hitting the ball over. Though his movements were silent, the music he played beat out through the ballpark, world singing to world.

———

I recalled a previous game against the Rays. Blake had gone through his ritual. When he was ready to bat, the Rays' pitcher let the first pitch go and hit Blake with the ball. The sound of the ball smacking Blake on the shoulder echoed through the park just as the sound of a stick echoes when it strikes a piñata; the impact, however, doesn't hurt a papier-mâché piñata nearly as much as it stings a young boy's shoulder. Blake was furious! Apparently the

Rays' pitcher had forgotten in whose universe he was playing. An explanation was in order. Blake wheeled to face the pitcher.

"What do you think you're doing?!"

A great characteristic of Down syndrome is the total lack, the total disregard, of inhibition. Blake says exactly what he thinks. The question was completely legitimate in his universe; it was legitimate in anyone's universe. I've always been envious that Blake can say whatever he thinks without consequence. I had moved down the third baseline quickly to make sure he wasn't hurt. After he screamed at the pitcher, I wondered whether, rather than checking on Blake, I would be preventing an FABL Bronco Division melee. The moment had all the elements in place for Blake to rush the mound, but I was finally able to settle him and get him to first base.

When Blake moved from the Pinto Division to the Mustang Division, from the pitching machine to a live pitcher, his being hit was my biggest fear. I had no idea how he would react. But this was Little League baseball, and getting hit by a pitch was bound to happen. I weighed the risk. He enjoyed playing so much. As simple as it was, I prepared a plan for the worst-case scenario. If Blake got hit and wouldn't bat again, we would stop playing; if he still wanted to bat, we would keep going. There was, however, no way to plan for the immediate aftermath of his being hit. I was resigned to waiting for and managing the incident when it came. We were three games into his first Mustang season when it happened.

"OW!" he screamed as he danced from the batter's box.

"Are you okay, Blakey?" I was there quickly. It was a short trip from the third base coach's box. Blake looked up with tears, anger, hurt, frustration, and incredulity all in one. His eyes spoke each emotion simultaneously. I'd never seen so many different emotions with one look.

"Dad, he hit me!"

"I know, Blake. It's all right. He didn't do it on purpose. I bet it really hurt. But now you get to go to first base." Then the unexpected came.

"I don't want to!"

He had been standing near the backstop, behind home plate. I couldn't help but laugh. I wasn't laughing at Blake being hit. His reaction was so unpredictable, and so spontaneous. I'd learned to roll until I could figure out what he wanted, but there was the pressure of all eyes upon us. I tried to hurry him along.

"C'mon, Blake, let's go to first base. I'll go with you."

"No, I won't go!"

"Don't you want to run the bases? Hurry, everyone's waiting." Then the answer came.

"No. I want to bat. Please, Dad, just one more. Please!"

In an instant, my fear of Blake being hit had disappeared. That same fear never existed, does not exist, inside Blake. I have never known anyone other than Blake who does not understand fear. The concept does not live in his world. Even today, every time Blake steps to the plate, he fully expects to hit the ball. That he could be hit by a pitch doesn't occur to him. He can't communicate it, but Blake has complete understanding of faith.

———

Now, watching "full ritual mode" in Blake's first at-bat in the championship game was a dream come true. *Full ritual mode* is burned into my memory. Blake was not intimidated as he stood at the plate. He swung the bat hard, swung at every pitch. The parents from both teams gave him terrific support, and though he couldn't generate a hit, he put on a great show as he played to the crowd. It was over far too quickly. Tony then came to the plate and landed on first base with a walk. Davey grounded out. Buck singled, scoring Johnny Coates, the fourth run of the inning. Unfortunately Seth, normally reliable at the plate, struck out with Tony at third and Buck at second. The top half of inning was over, but the Cubs had pushed four runs across the plate to tie, 4–4.

Chapter Twelve—Decision

Pitching again moved to the forefront. Baseball, at any age, at any level, is all about pitching. The rules allowed games last a maximum of six innings, unless the score was tied, with no new inning to begin after one hour and forty-five minutes; thus, the playing time that remained became the determining factor as I pondered pitching decisions. Pete could still pitch four more innings. Had that first one and a half innings taken long enough to justify pulling Davey and replacing him with Pete? I struggled, searching for resolution. I hesitated for a moment in the dugout. As I paused, Kristi seemed concerned.

"What are you waiting for?" she pressed.

"I'm trying to decide whether to make a pitching change now or to wait one more inning."

Kristi was anxious to discuss. Kristi loves the game. She can make tough decisions, and I value her counsel. We had made many decisions together about Blake, and about the entire family, choices that didn't involve baseball. Most of them were far more difficult than a timely pitching change.

———

Amanda was our first child. We anxiously awaited her birth. We settled on her name long before she was born. We counted the days, counted the minutes, before she came to us. I was so excited;

I mapped out the events leading to her birth well before the experience. I plotted it would be after midnight. Kristi would wake me in panic. We would grab her things and jump in the car. Amanda's delivery would be imminent. I would race to the hospital. I would ignore the speed limit in the rush, along with the enforcing officer and his patrol car's flashing lights. The officer would be intuitive. Instead of giving us a ticket, he would act as our escort. We would make it to the hospital just in time.

It didn't happen that way at all. Kristi called me at work about 10:00 AM. She said she was ready for delivery, but we didn't have to rush. We checked into the hospital and waited. The labor was long. It was 5:00 AM the next morning before Amanda entered the world. She was beautiful. As Dr. Jensen pulled her from the womb, he looked concerned. I watched him carefully. He put Amanda through the APGAR test. I didn't know how she was supposed to react, but I could tell she wasn't responding the way he expected. She looked fine to me, but I asked him if everything were all right. He told me he had some concerns and that he would return to address them. The hour we waited was one of the longest of our lives. He returned and explained he suspected Amanda was a child with Down syndrome. We had no idea there was any issue before she was born.

It was hard. It was so unexpected. There had to be a mistake. The genetic test came, and there was no mistake. We lashed out. We tried our own version of negotiation with God as we dealt with the emotion. The heavens seemed silent. We were discouraged. In the end, we accepted. Though I am ashamed I went through anger and grieving, there should be no shame. My process isn't much different than Blake's. There are no shortcuts; no one can change steps, in any universe. As we dealt with the difficulties of Amanda's birth, I called everyone I knew to tell them about her. I didn't want to relive the struggle each time I talked to someone who wasn't aware. After one such pronouncement, a good friend questioned us.

"What are you going to do?"

"What do you mean, what are we going to do?"

"Are you going to keep her?"

We dismissed him without any further discussion. Of course we would keep her. We have never even thought to look back. Amanda is wonderful, but more difficulty was on its way. We wanted more children. We consulted many wise physicians. Dr. Thomas, Amanda's pediatrician, gave us the best advice.

"What kind of baby do you want?"

We weren't quite sure what he was asking. You don't choose the baby born to you.

"That's my point. You can't choose if your baby has blonde hair and blue eyes. You decide to have a baby; then you accept the ramifications."

What were the ramifications? Kristi understood the specifics.

"I naturally spend more time with the kids than you do," she said. "If something goes wrong, I'm the one who will be judged. I'm willing to accept that judgment."

Never was that judgment more clear than when Kristi was pregnant with our second. She was five months along and running errands with one-year-old Amanda. She stepped into an office-building elevator with one other female occupant. As the elevator doors closed, the woman mumbled something to herself.

"Pardon me?" Kristi thought the woman was talking to her. Kristi had no idea of what was to come.

"I can't believe you would have the nerve to have another baby after you had one like *that!*"

How should Kristi have answered? It's easy to think of things to say without the pressure of the moment. The truth is that when such hurtful words come from out of nowhere, as these did, no one really knows what to say. Kristi hurriedly pressed the elevator floor buttons. In her anxiety, she probably hit every one. When the doors finally opened, she just got out.

The three of them were there together, Kristi standing, Amanda in her stroller, and Tyler in the womb, in an otherwise empty lobby. Kristi was in tears. But she loved, and she was loved. I wish I could have been there for her, for all three, in that moment. All I can do now is offer my profound respect. The children that followed Amanda are significant. Not one is a quarterback; not one throws a ninety-mile-per-hour fastball; not one is a beauty queen; but all contribute. All of them make the lives of those around them better. There is no one on this earth with the right to place an arbitrary value on their worth.

Tyler joined us. We loved Amanda and Tyler; we had tasted heaven. Could our universe expand? We considered. The worry through Kristi's pregnancy with Tyler had taken its toll. We were willing to accept any ramifications with a third child, but we didn't want surprises. We went to Kristi's OBGYN, Dr. Kelly. He assured us he could detect complications. Kristi made the difficult choice to move forward, and we were blessed with Blake. She loved him from the beginning.

As Blake entered his new universe, when I first laid eyes upon him, I knew he, just as Amanda, was a baby with Down syndrome. I was angry. I wasn't angry with Blake; I wasn't angry with Dr. Kelly; I wasn't angry with God. I was just angry. I didn't understand. I do understand now. Dr. Kelly hadn't missed anything. There were no complications. Kristi made a choice to deliver another baby like *that*, and the world is better for it.

———

As I thought about making a pitching change, Kristi broke the silence. "You need to wait one more inning. It's too early to make the change now."

I considered the four runs Davey had given up in the first inning. I glanced at my cell phone to check the time and pondered over the Rays' batting order. The next three Rays coming to bat were their three best hitters, and all three had already faced Davey once. Kristi was usually right when it came to family decisions. Perhaps I should have listened, but this was a baseball game.

"Let's make the change now. Pete, you go ahead and pitch."

Kristi was unbending. "You're changing him too early. You're making a mistake."

I continued to contemplate. I knew there was risk, but all things considered, the risk was warranted. Pete Henderson, wise beyond his twelve years, paused before he ran to the mound. He wasn't sure which way the discussion between husband and wife would turn. I clarified.

"What are you waiting for, Pete? It's your turn to pitch!"

There was a twinge of pleasant anxiety as Pete trotted to the mound. I love coaching, and I love being with the boys. The best thing about the whole process is making judgments void of the pressures Kristi and I feel when discussing family matters. Baseball is an escape. That Blake has achieved a level of success only adds to its pleasure. It's a rush to make a baseball decision and see the result. Sometimes it's a good choice, and it pays off. Sometimes it's foolish, and it hurts the team. The pleasure is watching it, pronouncement to fruition, independent of ramifications. This was a decision that would not bear fruit until the end of the game, four full innings from now. The result would be interesting.

Pete's first inning was not disappointing. He faced only three hitters and struck out two. The third hitter grounded out with a weak comebacker to the mound. The second inning ended with the score still tied, 4–4.

The top of the third inning was disappointing, although not lacking in drama. Pete started the inning with a single and moved around the bases to third. The inning continued as Justin and Sky both struck out. The Cubs needed to produce runs from the four and five spots in the batting order, which Justin and Sky filled on that day. Their failure to produce was opportunity lost. It was time for more tough decisions.

Collin was at the plate. Collin loved to swing the bat. Much to his lament, he was often called upon to bunt, but he always dutifully responded. Collin was the best bunter on the team, thus proving you don't need speed to lay down a good bunt. He had bunted in Chase from third base to score earlier in the season on a squeeze play. I considered using the squeeze once more. I gave the sign to both Pete and Collin. Pete's responsibility was to leave third base for home as soon as he knew the pitcher was throwing the pitch to the plate. Collin's responsibility was to get his bat on the ball no matter where the ball was. If he didn't make contact, the percentages were high that Pete would be tagged out by the catcher.

Collin looked up with disdain. "I want to hit the ball!" he screamed with his eyes. His nonverbal caused concern, but it didn't change anything. The Cubs needed the run; Collin needed to bunt. I waited to see what would happen. Justin took off toward home as the pitcher let go of the ball. Collin squared his bat around, but the pitch was high and difficult to reach. He made no effort to make contact with the ball. It had been explained over and over again that a squeeze play required the bunter to make contact, no matter where the pitch was thrown. Collin watched the ball go by, putting the runner in great jeopardy. The Rays' catcher caught the baseball and lunged toward Pete. Pete dodged around the catcher's tag, out of the baseline, and stepped on home plate. The umpire called him safe; the Rays' coaches came rushing from their dugout.

"He was out of the baseline!" Ted screamed. "You have to call him out!"

Pete did run out of the baseline, and he should have been called out, but experience taught me that with a close call made to my benefit, the most important thing was to restore play as quickly as possible. It didn't make sense to argue a favorable decision; as soon as play resumed, there was generally no reversing.

"Way to go, Pete!" I yelled.

Pete paused to listen to the Rays' coaches argue the call. It looked as if he wanted to get involved. I talked to Pete again.

"He called you safe, Pete. Go sit down. Step up to the plate, Collin, and finish your at-bat."

Ted didn't give up without a fight, but the umpire stood by his call. As the argument finished, Collin looked sheepishly back at me. There was no reprimand. He could tell by my tone toward the umpire that I was disappointed. His expression reflected that he comprehended. He understood the consequence of not putting the bat on the ball during a squeeze play. He wouldn't make the same mistake again.

Fortunately, Pete scored for the Cubs; unfortunately, Collin's emotions were ebbing, and he finished the at-bat meekly by striking out. The top half of the third inning ended with the Cubs ahead 5–4.

Chapter Thirteen—Destruction

In Blake's universe, the bottom half of the inning displayed the propensity for catastrophic events. The Rays were at the top of their batting order. Pete started strong, striking out the Rays' leadoff hitter, but he walked the number two hitter, and the number three hitter reached base when the catcher dropped the ball on a called third strike, allowing the hitter to run for first. That put runners at both first and second. Pete had a good move to first. He had bailed out the team before by picking off base runners. Not this time. Pete held his foot to the side of the rubber and went into his stretch. He brought the ball down to his chest, into his glove, and stopped. Without moving his head, he wheeled toward first base and let the ball go. Justin, our first baseman, missed the throw. The runners advanced to second and third as the ball rolled out of play. Ted came out of the dugout again. I was bothered as I watched him rush toward the umpire. A trend was emerging. After a brief discussion, sure enough, the ump signaled the runners to continue one more base.

There was confusion. The old rule of one base on an overthrow should have applied. Pete had been in the stretch with his foot on the pitching rubber when he made the throw to first. The runners should have been allowed to advance only one base. Ted argued successfully that both runners were entitled to an additional base. I wasn't sure about the rule; intuitively I felt as if the call were incorrect. Unfortunately, some of the Cubs' parents were positive the call was wrong, and that started an unrelenting attack on the umpire.

Destructive forces have always existed in the universe. Evidence that meteors have pummeled the moon is clearly visible; that the sun's heat incinerates anything that approaches too closely is irrefutable; that the gravity of black holes never releases any unfortunate object is undeniable. As to Little League baseball, attacking a fifteen-year-old umpire leads to similar destruction. There isn't any place for it, not in an ordered world.

Sky's dad ran onto the field, screaming at the umpire. "That is *not* the right call! The base runners *do not* advance!" Meteors rained down on the Farmington Bronco Field.

Stunning! Naive though it may have been, I didn't expect this level of intensity at a baseball game. It was almost as intense as little league football. Sky's dad was an intimidating figure to a young boy; he would be to anyone. He wasn't tall, but he was big, and he was aggressive. I wondered what to do. I wasn't sure about the call, and I was concerned the Cubs' parents might feel abandoned if I didn't get in the middle of it.

The confrontation was deeply troubling. No young umpire deserved to be yelled at. It made no sense to scream at a fifteen-year-old over a baseball game. On the other hand, what if the incorrect call had been made? Over the years, I developed a reputation as one of the calmest coaches in the league when dealing with players and umpires. It wasn't a reputation I sought; it just didn't seem right to scream at a boy doing his best umpiring other boys. Was my reticence hurting the team? Sky's dad had worn his fire-engine red Red Sox baseball jersey. It made him appear as big as the sun. He verbally turned to ash any object that approached. The umpire ejected him. It was a good decision; order needed to be restored. Sky's dad grudgingly complied but only after he uttered a few more "instructions" to the umpire. Then

Tony's dad, Chris Jacobson, piped up. He did not advance on the umpire while he spoke; he stayed in his seat.

"The call to advance the runners is wrong," he said firmly, and he did not relent.

Just as space debris being sucked into the black hole's vortex, the confrontation seemed to build on its own momentum. The umpire approached. Consumed with the events, I didn't notice the boy until he came close. He looked at me, pleading, though tear-filled eyes. Correct call or not, I felt for him.

"Coach, I'm going to call the game if you can't control your parents."

"You just need to relax. I'll take care of my parents, but you just need to relax. You're doing fine. It will all work out." I then approached Chris. "I just need to ask you guys to calm down, or the boy will call the game."

Chris looked up and responded. "The boy shouldn't even be in this position," he said. "Here we are, in a championship game, and there is no league official in the park. How can you play a championship game without a league official here? It really is ridiculous."

Chris was right. There should have been a league official at the game. I walked away from the umpire in the field and approached the home plate umpire.

"We need a league official here before we can continue," I calmly told the other boy. "This is a championship game, and there is no official. I don't understand that."

A spectator came out from the crowd, looking for an argument.

"Come on, Coach. Why don't you go back to your dugout and quit arguing with the umps? All you've been doing the entire game is arguing."

His comments were comical. As I have said, I had the reputation for not abusing players and umpires. Adults who didn't know what they were talking about were a different matter. I obliged.

"What game have you been watching?" I demanded. "I haven't argued any calls at all. I didn't argue this call, and I haven't argued any calls before this one. I only came to make sure a league official is here so problems like these can be stopped before they start. Maybe you ought to watch more closely."

He was silenced. He hung his head and skulked silently back into the crowd.

———

Blake had seen this kind of destruction before. The devastation affects him, but it is not the crushing act that causes him to feel. His sensitivities are intuitive and are based upon others' feelings. He senses the struggle through Kristi and me. He then reveals his own internal struggle with an emotional display. Emotions that are unprocessed do not spontaneously dissipate. Perhaps the damage is more evident in my world than in the one where Blake is the center.

We didn't have trouble when we initially took Blake for haircuts. Oh, he wasn't perfect; he is, after all, a boy. He was wiggly and impatient. But he wasn't any different from any other little boy getting a haircut, and he wasn't bad. On a beautiful Saturday, Kristi took him to the cut salon for his usual trim. Assuming all was well, she entered the shop happily.

"Hi. I'm here to get Blake a haircut."

From behind the counter, the female manager answered tersely. "Well, will he be good?"

"What is that supposed to mean?"

"I'll only let a boy like *that* get a haircut here if he's good."

I'm not sure what it is with the world and a boy like *that*. Kristi left the salon in tears. No one, neither the son nor the mother, deserves such treatment. After Kristi related the incident to me, I called the owner. He was defiant.

"I don't think my manager did anything wrong."

"What do you mean she didn't do anything wrong?"

"She doesn't have to cut anyone's hair who can't behave."

"How could she know he wouldn't behave? She refused him before she even tried."

Later that day, I got a phone call from a beautician who worked at the salon and watched the entire episode.

"I saw how the manager treated your wife and little boy. I'm ashamed of what she did. I've already quit. I'll verify the incident with anyone you want. No one should be treated in that way."

I placed one more call to the owner. He was still uncooperative.

"I told you my manager didn't do anything wrong. Why are you calling me again?"

I'm no lawyer, but I've learned in this type of situation to never ask a question to which I don't already know the answer.

"Are all the beauticians who were working that day still working at your salon?"

Apparently, the owner of the salon was an attorney. He had learned to answer while divulging as little information as possible.

"No."

"There have been changes?"

"One quit."

"That's interesting. Do you know why?"

"She wasn't happy."

"Maybe I can add a little detail. She saw the treatment the manager gave my wife and my son. She didn't want to be associated with someone so cruel. She will confirm the entire incident. You know I could press a civil suit; you know I would win. It just doesn't mean that much to me. But you ought to think long and hard about the people that work for you."

The owner made no change at his salon. Kristi was deeply hurt. From then on, haircuts were left to me. I tried to forget, I tried to not hold a grudge, but I'm not as good at it as Blake. We were fortunate enough to find another salon that would cut the hair of a boy like *that*. With each visit, I tried to bury my anxiety, but the scars of such impacts are slow to crumble. I tried to hide from Blake the fear I felt each time we walked through the salon door. He didn't understand, but he knew. He sensed. It wasn't until I processed my own emotions that he was also able to let go.

As the spectator skulked back into the crowd, Ryan West, the league president, appeared. "I'm here," he said.

"That's all I wanted." I walked toward the team so play could resume. As I entered the dugout, Blake stopped me.

"What's wrong, Dad?"

Blake was watching. He knew I was mad. His knowledge wasn't based on what I had said. He sensed how I felt. With Blake, there is no way to hide emotions behind a facade. Whether I'm angry or calm, he knows. There isn't any way to fake it. I needed to deal with my emotions quickly. Blake's intuitive abilities, and the consequences that follow, can never be underestimated.

As I considered, the game's import suddenly changed. I could not discount the elation I felt for Blake and the sense of accomplishment we would share when he was presented his trophy. But at that moment, his achievement seemed less meaningful. The confrontation between parent and umpire had pushed that achievement into the outer reaches of the universe, disappearing into perception's nebulae. The parents of *the many* were asserting their collective will, focusing on the game's score rather than on the accomplishments of their sons.

I felt myself being pulled. I didn't know if I could extinguish the firestorm smoldering within me. For the first time that evening, I wondered if it were enough to just be playing in the championship game. Vince Lombardi once said, "Winning isn't everything; it's the only thing."

Blake then innocently smiled to me. He spoke again.

"What he say, Dad?"

Truth and light then broke through the haze. Lombardi was right! I wanted to win! But the win I hoped for was in seeing boys become good men. I love baseball, but more important victories are to be had than those measured by a score. It had everything to do with playing baseball, very little to do with the game's scoreboard.

"I'm great, Blakey. Let's play!"

Blake smiled to me again, this time with his eyes, and went about finding a batting helmet. I couldn't hide how I felt from Blake. I've learned to not even try. I really was okay. I'd faced my anger, and the situation had been resolved. The inning had been difficult. The Rays scored four runs to take an 8–5 lead. It didn't matter. It was a simple genesis.

Chapter Fourteen—Healing

Powerful forces wreak havoc in the universe. But then the grandeur, the magnificence, the beauty of the universe asserts itself. In the wake of destruction, healing rises. The game continued. Johnny Coates singled to reach first base, beginning the healing process where meteors rained. After Blake and Tony struck out, Davey came through with a big hit to score Johnny. The ash settled. Batting next, Buck hit a slow-rolling grounder to third, used his great speed, and beat out the throw to first for an infield single. That moved Davey to third base, and Seth singled to score Davey. Objects adjusted their movements according to the absolutes and avoided the black hole.

Although he struck out, Blake contributed greatly to the healing process. He was excited as he came to the plate. He looked at me with purpose.

"Dad, I going to hit the ball far."

———

In Einstein's universe, time is relative. In Blake's universe, both time *and* space are relative. As to time, amazingly, Blake sees everything in the present. There is no past, and there is no future. Time is rolled into one great whole. That contributes to why he never fears the pitched ball when he stands at bat. He remembers every hit. Although those hits happened in *our* past, they exist in *his* now. As for the painful at-bats, he has emotionally processed them through his consciousness. He remembers them, but he doesn't. He filters the pain. Blake does not see the future. He does not predict future events, but in his Down syndrome way, he moves future events to the present.

His vision is both rewarding and frustrating. The positive is that he focuses on the good. The difficultly is with the future. I must be very careful when I tell Blake we have a baseball game. He puts his uniform on immediately. It can be a problem when I've told him two days in advance. He won't take his uniform off until after the game. When we travel, Blake sees only the destination rather than the journey. Questions such as "How much further?" or "Are we there yet?" seem to never end. Waiting for Christmas morning is unbearable. I know other boys show the same enthusiasm, but Blake's eagerness rises from his differing vision. The absolutes have taught ways around these problems. I wait until a couple of hours before game time before I tell Blake to get ready to play. When we prepare him for travel, we include the journey as part of the destination. Time questions are answered with a completion time differing from his expectation. Whether accurate or not, it usually satisfies. For him, it moves the event to the now.

As to space, his relative understanding is humorous. He has no concept of space. Blake tries to hide things that can't be hidden. Along with chips, Blake loves cheese puffs. Kristi will buy the big, clear, five-gallon containers from time to time for a treat. She had done just that on a Saturday trip to the store. Blake knew he wasn't supposed to take the cheese puffs from the pantry, but the temptation was too great. He wanted cheese puffs while he watched TV. He sneaked the puffs into the great room and ate his fill. Later that same afternoon, I went searching. The puffs weren't in the pantry. It didn't take long to deduce who had taken them. I figured I'd give Blake fair warning before I caught him with the evidence.

"Blake, do you know where the cheese puffs are?"

There was a rustle before I entered the room. I waited until the dust had settled, and then I opened the door.

"Hi, Blake. Did you hear me? Do you know where the cheese puffs are?"

Blake shrugged his shoulders.

"I don't know."

I couldn't help but laugh at what I saw. Blake had hidden the cheese puffs, five-gallon jar and all, under the couch cushion. Rather than in its proper place, the couch cushion was vertical. Blake truly believed I wouldn't be able to see the cheese puffs under the vertical cushion. He wouldn't admit guilt until I held the jar directly in front of him.

———

When Blake said he was going to hit the ball far, I was confident. He remembered the times he hit the ball successfully. He had already filtered the destructive forces of the game out of his mind. On this day, he had come to play baseball. The first pitch came, and just as Casey, Blake swung with all his might. Again, just as Casey, Blake hit only air.

"No!"

He stormed out of the batter's box and looked toward me. I gave him a stern look, telling him to settle down without speaking. He regained composure in his Down syndrome way and stepped back into the box; then he raised his hand to call time out. He looked the pitcher in the eye.

"You throw it *right* here."

He pointed with his bat to exactly where he wanted the ball thrown. The Rays' pitcher complied. Blake's swing came down on the ball, and he made contact. The ball flew high down the left field line and then sadly disappeared. It traveled behind the dugout and over the out-of-play fence. Blake had been struggling at the plate. Hitting the pitching of a twelve-year-old had proven to be far more difficult than hitting that of a ten-year-old. He felt the contact, briefly watched the flight of the ball, and then dropped his bat and ran excitedly for first base. To suggest that Blake's gait was fluid would not be accurate. The gait was ungainly; in his universe, however, it was in perfect rhythm and in perfect flow. It is the most beautiful stride I have seen. I followed him to first base.

"That was a great hit, Blake! You did hit the ball far. The ball went foul; you get another chance."

"But, Dad," he pleaded, "I hit the ball over the fence!"

"Yes, you did. Let's go back and see if you can do it one more time."

Blake was satisfied with another opportunity to take a swing at the ball. His concept of space excluded foul and out-of-play. Because he had already made contact, it was a free turn. He happily walked back to the plate and readied himself in the box.

"Strike three!" the umpire yelled as the pitch crossed the plate. This time he was careful not to say "You're out!" That was left to me. I was there quickly to help Blake avoid any problem.

"That was strike three, Blake. You have to go to the dugout." In Blake's universe, time's relative nature then asserted itself.

"But, Dad," he pleaded. His hand gestures were distinctly Blake. He extended both arms out with his palms up. His arms moved up and down to the cadence of his speech. "I hit the ball far. I hit it over the fence!"

"Yes, you did. It was a great hit. You'll get to bat again later."

Just being with Blake can soothe and calm. Even when he does something he shouldn't, he makes it difficult to be angry. His hold on innocence, coupled with his ability for mischief, is unmatched.

Blake has celiac disease. He can't eat anything with gluten. It's complicated, but it means he can't eat *anything* containing wheat. The diet is very difficult to follow. Wheat is in just about every prepared food available. The problem is compounded by the diet's blandness. We wrestled with what to do about Blake's new diet, especially what to do for Tyler. Would we impose the diet on Tyler, or would we find ways to cook two different meals—one gluten-filled, the other gluten-free—every time we ate? Tyler is isolated in so many ways. We didn't want to make his isolation even more difficult by imposing a gluten-free diet on the family. Okay, maybe I'm the one who can't handle the gluten-free diet. At any rate, Blake's health and longevity depend upon it. Thus, we are forced to have two menus in our home.

In his Down syndrome way, Blake understands the diet's complications. He tries to stick to the regimen, but he is Blake. From time to time, there are breakdowns. Come Kristi's birthday, she wanted chocolate cake. We'd bought a can of prepared frosting for the cake. It's loaded with gluten. I sneaked the frosting into the pantry; I thought I'd hidden it well. When it comes to food in the house, however, Blake is omniscient. Armed with his most powerful weapon, the spoon, he found the frosting and finished off the entire can in one sitting. He didn't have the best aim as he ate. When he was finished, he had chocolate frosting all over his face. He wore a clown's makeup around his mouth. The only difference was, rather than red grease paint, it was chocolate.

As he sought to destroy the evidence, he stumbled upon Kristi. She immediately knew what had taken place. Blake wore the story all over his face. But he wasn't about to go down without a fight.

"Blake, whatcha doin'?" she asked, rhythmically.

He stood in front of her, arms behind his back, kicking his foot as if his toe were in the sand. "Nuttin'," he answered, in kind.

It was all she could do to keep from laughing, but she had to see it through. She wiped the smile from her face and asked again, this time more forcibly.

"Blake, what are you doing?"

He still wouldn't give in. "Nothing," he said as he shrugged his shoulders.

She took a deep breath, and gathered herself one more time.

"Blake Curtis! What are you doing?"

"Oh, all right. Frosting!" Then he stormed away.

Blake's ability to process has a downside. Once the trouble is left behind, he quickly forgets; the riptide leaves no residual. It is difficult to connect consequences and actions. It also makes it hard to stay mad at him for any length of time.

I can't be angry.

———

As everyone watched Blake, calm again settled on the Farmington Bronco Field. Blake was satisfied too. Knowing he would have another turn was enough. He turned toward the dugout. I envy Blake. Though he tries constantly to improve, he does not overreach. He knows who he is, and he is comfortable and confident. Blake has a greater understanding of what really does bring joy than anyone I know. The healing process was complete.

Pete Henderson came to the plate. He uncharacteristically struck out, ending the inning. The score was now 8–7 moving to the bottom of the fourth.

Pete then settled down to pitch. He faced three hitters, and he struck out all three. After four complete innings, the score was still 8–7 for the Rays, and the middle of the order for the Cubs was coming to the plate. The time limit for the game was approaching, and the umpire came over to talk.

"Unless there is a tie, this is the last inning, Coach."

Ironically, it was also the last inning Pete Henderson was available to pitch. Kristi overheard the conversation with the umpire. I seized the opportunity.

"Is this the time to tell you I made the pitching change at *exactly* the right time?"

She was playfully angry as she smiled and answered.

"You're a jerk."

It had been fun to make decisions during the game and great to see them work. Every move had gone according to plan. At some point, however, one needs to realize to not press his luck. After the timeliness of the pitching change was pointed out, the subject was dropped, and focus redirected to the team. Justin led off the inning with a single. Sky and Collin followed by striking out, and then Johnny Coates came to bat. Justin was a great base runner. He had worked his way to third base with intelligent base running and was poised to score.

The moment was intense. There were two outs; if the Cubs couldn't push Justin across the plate, the game would be over.

Chapter Fifteen—Hesitation

Many love baseball for the strategy of the game. When do you steal? When do you walk a batter? When do you bunt? Those components are important, and they make the game worthwhile. Observing the development of those strategies, intuitively applied through a young boy's mind, is one of the joys of coaching. Throughout the season, many of the Cubs had developed their intuitive baseball skills. Johnny Coates was not among them. Second only to Collin in his ability to bunt, Johnny lagged behind in understanding when to lay the bunt down. With Justin at third, a timely bunt brought the strong possibility of scoring a run. I sensed Johnny wouldn't lay the ball down. I calculated. Johnny had missed an earlier tournament game. After that game, I called his mom to make sure everything was okay. It wasn't.

"Johnny is worried he will be the one who makes the team lose," she told me. "He was in the car, and we made it all the way to the park, but he wouldn't get out for the game. We ended up going home."

"Let me talk to him," I pleaded. "Of course we want him at the game. He needs to be a part of the team."

She did not relent. "No, it would be better if you didn't talk to him right now. I will make sure he comes to the game though. He'll be ready to play."

It was a difficult situation. I wondered what I had missed. I couldn't remember anything I might have done to embarrass Johnny. He had broken his collarbone playing soccer early in the season and returned to the team later. He had some catching up to do, but he had learned. I tried to help him join the rhythm of the team, but clearly I hadn't been as successful as I thought. Johnny was here now and seemed to be enjoying himself. It was the perfect time to bunt, but as I plotted, I knew he wouldn't bunt on his own. There were two outs, and the game-tying run was at third. A well-executed bunt, of which he was capable, would score Justin and send the game to extra innings. This was an instance, however, although the *one* was not Blakey, that the needs of the one outweighed the needs of the many. I met Johnny at the plate, and we walked away from the Rays' dugout. When we were out of earshot, I knelt to his height.

"This would be a good time to bunt, don't you think?"

"I think I'd rather try to just hit the ball."

I considered the game; I considered the absolutes. "You go ahead and hit it. Bash it to the fence."

Johnny gave me a relieved smile. He stepped into the batter's box as I returned to coach third base.

As Johnny prepared to hit, Justin, who had developed some intuition of his own, silently communicated his desire to steal home. We planned on waiting one pitch. On the second pitch maybe we would try a passed-ball steal, maybe we would try a squeeze. Words were spoken, but they were minimal. We both quietly understood. There was no way the game would end with the potential game-tying run on third base. Unfortunately, no squeeze was coming.

The earth rotates on its axis continually. What would happen if it stood still? What would happen if its motion hesitated? Are there actions committed by men, whether they have positive or negative impact on others, that can actually stop its rotation? It depends on whose universe the earth is in.

I wasn't the only one plotting. The Rays' pitcher watched closely as Ted quickly moved his right hand across his chest, to the brim of his cap, and then to his belt. The hand to the belt was the indicator sign, the sign that his next movement would be the instruction for the coming pitch. Ted then moved his hand to his back. The significance of the movement was lost to everyone at the ballpark except the pitcher. At that moment, the rotation of the earth hesitated. Ted had signaled his pitcher to hit Johnny Coates on purpose, thus sending him to first base.

In Blake's universe, the earth stopped.

There is nothing wrong with the stratagem of purposely hitting a batter to put him on base. For a different reason, to help my pitcher, I used the same strategy earlier in the game. Sometimes a stronger hitter is put on base to bring a weaker hitter to the plate for an easier out. But this time it was Blake who was sucked into the vortex; Blake Curtis, the only player with Down syndrome to ever play in the FABL, was coming to the plate next, brought by design as the weak hitter with two outs and a runner on third. Blake Curtis might possibly be the last batter for his team in the championship game. Not just any ball game, the championship game at the center of the universe. Ted was doing everything he could to help his team win. Apparently no one had explained to Ted the concept of a mockingbird, of justice, in Blake's universe. The Rays' pitcher correctly read the sign. His first pitch of the at-bat hit Johnny on the foot, sending Johnny to first base. Now Blakey was coming to the plate.

As Blake strode in his ungainly gait toward the batter's box, time bent. No one intercepted and deciphered the Rays' signals. No one could prove Johnny was hit intentionally, but I knew what Ted had done. I mumbled to myself. There were some swear words involved, but I'm not going to write them here.

"I can't believe he just did that."

I was angry, and then I stopped. The wonder of the entire evening caught up with me. I wanted to hold the scent from the hot dogs at the concession, just to taste their smell; I wanted to hang on the aroma of the freshly watered infield, just to hold its purity; I wanted one more passing of the evening breeze across my farmer-tanned face. That Blake stood at the plate with so much at stake invoked awe. This was the at-bat, the one at-bat that every father dreams of; this was the at-bat with the game's outcome hanging in the balance, the at-bat with two outs and the tying run beckoning at third base. My own son, my son with Down syndrome, was coming to the plate.

I've always been a bit of a romantic. A line by the Tigers' pitcher, Billy Chapel, from the movie *For Love of the Game* flowed into my mind.

> God, I always said I would never bother you about baseball. Lord knows you have bigger things to worry about. But if you could make this pain in my shoulder stop for ten minutes, I would really appreciate it.[6]

Some may disagree with Chapel's plea. I always felt God would happily involve Himself in a baseball game. God's involvement might not be, however, what the prayer offerer desires, but seeing the result, as opposed to the offerer's wish, might add insight into the operation of any universe. Desiring divine intervention was easy; avoiding asking God for an unfair advantage for Blakey was far more difficult. I wrestled with what to do. I loved Blakey, and this was only a baseball game.

It would be great to pinch-hit for Blake, I thought. *But Blake deserves just as much opportunity to play, maybe more, than anyone. Plus, if I do pinch-hit for him, I probably won't be able to go home after the game.*

---

6   "Three More," *For Love of the Game*, directed by Sam Raimi (Universal City, CA: Universal Pictures, 1999), DVD.

Although I couldn't know at the time, Kristi, sitting behind home plate and watching Blakey come to bat, was thinking, *I wish he'd pinch-hit for Blake right now so if he gets out no one will think it's his fault we lose.*

The decision was difficult. It shouldn't have been. Blake had done nothing but make music for all who would listen.

In *To Kill a Mockingbird*, Scout described protecting a man, a mockingbird. The story presents Sheriff Tate's defense of Arthur "Boo" Radley after Bob Ewell's death. Boo led his entire life in seclusion, afraid to come out of his house, afraid to come out from the shadows. Boo never harmed anyone, but rumors abounded about his mental status and nature.

Men fear what they do not understand.

On Halloween night in 1935, Boo came out of his house for the last time. He came out to protect the only two friends he had ever known, although he only knew them from afar. Boo came out to save the lives of Jem and Scout Finch. In the process, Bob Ewell was killed.

> Mr. Tate was trying to dig a hole in the floor with the toe of his boot. He pulled his nose, then he massaged his left arm. "I may not be much, Mr. Finch, but I'm still sheriff of Maycomb County and Bob Ewell fell on his knife. Good night, sir."
>
> Mr. Tate stamped off the porch and strode across the front yard. His car door slammed and he drove away.
>
> Atticus sat looking at the floor for a long time. Finally he raised his head. "Scout," he said, "Mr. Ewell fell on his knife. Can you possibly understand?"
>
> Atticus looked like he needed cheering up. I ran to him and hugged him and kissed him with all my might. "Yes sir, I understand," I reassured him. "Mr. Tate was right."

Atticus disengaged himself and looked at me. "What do you mean?"

"Well, it'd be sort of like shootin' a mockingbird, wouldn't it?"[7]

There would be no eclipse. Blake would bat. The Cubs would win or lose the game with Blake at the plate. There would be no pinch hitter for him on this day. He had earned his turn. What he had not earned, however, was the responsibility of the fate of so many worlds being placed upon his shoulders; what he had not earned was the earth spinning on his ability to hit a baseball.

In that instant, time stood still. For that moment, my son, my son with Down syndrome, was the center of every universe intersecting at the Farmington Bronco Field. All eyes were focused on him. I never thought it possible. Dreams come true.

The magnitude of the moment escaped Blake. Each at-bat was the same to him. When he came to hit, those who were really watching were able to see everything good about Little League baseball, about being a boy. From the tapping of his spikes to the pointing to the field where he intended to hit the ball, Blake reveled in every moment of playing the game, of playing the game created for boys. He was oblivious that the parents of every Cub player held their collective breath for him. They hoped, as his father hoped, that he would deliver the game-tying hit. He was unaware that the parents of every Rays' player were bitterly torn. They were torn between their desire to see Blake succeed and their desire to see one more out, the out that would finish, finish in their favor, the game played at the center of the universe. Blake did not know Johnny Coates had been intentionally hit so the Rays could pitch to him.

In that moment, that oblivion was Blake's most important trait; he just wanted to hit the baseball.

---

7   Lee, *To Kill a Mockingbird*, 318.

I caught Justin's eye one more time. He understood. He was going home on a straight steal on the next pitch. I always hoped to be there in the moment Justin's potential and performance met. I'm not talking about baseball. Though he was only twelve, through some miracle of maturity, in that moment Justin considered Blake more than he did himself. He didn't want Blake to fail. He was willing to sacrifice himself for Blake, a sacred gift, even if the medium was just a baseball game. Albeit briefly, the broader view of the universe was opened, magically opened to him, through baseball's vision. He left third base just as the pitcher made his motion toward home. He didn't have a great jump from third, but it didn't matter.

It would have been noble if I had sent Justin home to "steal" a mockingbird, to save the game in order to protect Blake, as Sheriff Tate had protected Boo Radley. Sometimes, however, nobility is buried in sheer competitiveness. The truth was I wanted to do everything I could for all the boys, all my boys including and especially Blake, so they could win the championship.

There is no way we are going to finish with the tying run on third, I thought again as I watched Justin break for home. The pitch was outside and in the dirt. The ball slid by the catcher as Justin crossed the plate. The game was tied!

The earth was spinning again. Order was restored to Blake's universe. So many worlds; on the move, once more.

Blakey struck out to finish the Cubs' at-bat. I didn't care. His performance was a cosmic event, a harmony of the worlds.

Chapter Sixteen—Participation

The Cubs had put together enough runs to tie the score. Now it was up to Pete to close out the side. Ted came to me as Pete walked toward the mound.

"You can't pitch Pete this inning. You pitched him four innings in the last game, and this will be his fourth this game. That adds up to eight innings; you need to make a change."

I looked at Ted and laughed. He had acted as the league official throughout the game, but it must not have been enough. Now he was trying to determine my pitching rotation. "Sorry, Coach," I said. "Pete only pitched three innings last game. He still has one more inning to pitch."

There was no argument. Though not completely convinced the number of innings Pete pitched was accurate, Ted left for his dugout to prepare his team. The game moved forward. Pete's pitching didn't disappoint anyone supporting the Cubs. He struck out the first three hitters he faced, but had to face a fourth, for the second batter of the inning reached first base when the catcher dropped the ball on a called third strike. He struck the fourth batter out also, and the Cubs ran to their dugout to prepare for their second consecutive extra-inning game, with the score tied 8–8.

Tony started off the inning with a walk. He reached second base on a passed ball while Davey was batting, and then Davey struck out. Buck came to the plate and went to first with a walk. Then both he and Tony moved one base on a double-steal. Seth hit a fly to center to score Tony, and the Cubs led 9–8. Pete was thrown out at first to end the top half of the inning.

Deciding whom to pitch then became easy. Seth was the only experienced pitcher left to send to the mound. He was available for six innings; he had only pitched in one inning to that point. Though he had struggled, no one was concerned. Seth pitched his best in relief situations, with the game on the line. The bottom of the sixth inning began with the heart of the Rays' order (the four and five hitters) coming to the plate.

The leadoff hitter doubled to begin. He moved to third base on a steal. Losing the game on a passed ball by the catcher would be unforgivable. Time was called while we shifted Pete to catcher. Sky came in from the outfield to play third base, and Buck moved to shortstop. Seth threw a couple of pitches while I considered the infield alignment. The Cubs were missing their regular second baseman, Jared Wise, and their regular shortstop, Chase Everett, both out of town for the tournament. The team had made due, but the lack of a quality infield had taken its toll. Buck was the best infielder the Cubs had left after Pete went to catcher, hence his playing shortstop. The problem was third base. Seth, pitching from the right side and facing third in his stretch, enjoyed trying to pick off base runners at the hot corner. Third was the bigger risk. I called another time-out, and Buck moved back to third. Sky was now playing shortstop.

The next batter ripped a liner right at shortstop. Sky raised his glove to protect his face and found the ball tucked inside. In a moment of good fortune, he had been paying attention to the game. At the end of the contest, a parent from the Rays commented moving Sky to shortstop as brilliant. The parents' impression was Sky had been moved because he was the better infielder. I didn't have the heart to explain the move had been made to protect third base. It really is better to be lucky than good. The number six hitter came to the plate and singled to score the runner from third. After that, Seth settled down. He retired the next two batters he faced. The first extra inning had ended with the score tied 9–9. The game moved to the top of the seventh.

Justin led off by striking out. Sky followed by tripling to the gap in right-center field. It was a great hit, and with one out, the chance for Sky to score was high. Unfortunately Sky did not have Justin's baseball savvy. There was no opportunity for Sky to try to steal home. It was up to either Collin or Johnny Coates to get a base hit to score him. Unfortunately, neither Collin nor Johnny made contact with the ball. The Cubs' half of the seventh inning ended with the score still tied at 9.

I was irritated, my world in commotion. I felt myself slipping again into perception's haze. Great opportunity had been wasted. I wanted to finish the game myself. Didn't the Cubs know how important this game was? Were they doing everything they could to win? Couldn't they understand how much it meant? For crying out loud, we were playing extra innings in the championship game at the center of the universe! What would it take to push one more run across the plate?

"Hi, Dad! What's up?"

It was Amanda. Her cherubic face was pressed into the chain link fence as she spoke.

"How's the game going?"

Aristotle held that the earth was the center of the universe. He devised a complex series of spheres to account for the orbits of the solar system. Later, Copernicus studied the same orbits. Rather than the earth as its center, he presented a model of the universe with the sun at its hub to account for those orbits. How could

Aristotle have missed such a fundamental component of the universe? How could two of the most brilliant men of their respective times see something so differently? It doesn't matter that both were wrong. Universal truth is not arbitrary; universal truth is not subjective; universal truth is not perception. There are times that someone who sees with perspective and with clarity must open our view; then we are able to see things as they really are.

"Hi, Amanda."

"We've been here a long time." She pulled me into her world. "Can I get a hot dog?"

"Sure." I dragged a crumpled dollar from my pocket and handed it to her. As she smoothed it, she spoke.

"Thanks, Dad. Can I put ketchup on it?" Amanda has diabetes. Ketchup is a big deal.

"Sure. Ask Mom to give you a shot."

"Thanks, Dad. Good luck with your game!"

My game? How could I be so selfish? For the second time that evening, one of my children with Down syndrome brought clarity to the ballpark. I was not the center of every universe, and this game was Blake's. For that matter, it was Amanda's too. I smiled to Amanda, properly rebuked.

The bottom of the seventh was uneventful. Seth faced the last three hitters of the Rays' batting order and struck out all three. The second extra inning ended with the score still tied at 9. The top of the eighth, the third extra inning, started out difficultly for the Cubs. Blake came to the plate first. It was his fourth at-bat in the championship game. It was also to be his last at-bat on that magical night. He had played almost seven hours of marathon baseball, and it was beginning to show.

"Dad, I tired."

"You're up to bat, Blakey."

That was all he needed. He was on his feet, ready for his turn. He strode to the plate and readied for the first pitch. It was exceptionally dark for a summer evening. A heavy blanket of clouds had rolled up against the mountains east of Farmington, covering the stars. As Blake strode to the plate and readied for the first pitch, the field lights shone down upon him. It was as if he were on a stage, with the spotlight directed only on him. His Cubs' uniform jersey, #9 on his back, fit perfectly. His tight gray baseball pants showed the strength of his legs. His blue Cubs' hat with the red *C* in front was identical to the hats all the boys wore. But it was *his* uniform.

———

It had been nearly a year since that magical night. Aubree is our youngest, the *Little One*. She got her nickname from C.S. Lewis's *The Chronicles of Narnia*. She earned it because of her gentleness and kindness - at least when she was five. Unfortunately, those traits were not the entire reason for the nickname. Aubree wouldn't let me call her *Baby Girl* any more. It must have had something to do with her fifth birthday. She is growing up, all too fast. I had to come up with something different to appease her. Someday I'll write a book about her, but first she has to live her life. The day will come soon enough.

Aubree had a baseball practice, and I was fortunate enough to be there. As I was watching her with her friends, I was feeling sorry for myself. Blake was playing baseball again. I was coaching his team, and the team was struggling. We lost on opening day, 24–5. At the time of Aubree's practice, Blake's new team, the Yankees, had an 0–3 record. Aubree was learning the rhythm of the game. It is never easy. There must have been a magnet inside the ball her team used at practice, its polarity opposite to little boys and little girls. The ball's magnetic effect was stunning. The Dodgers, Aubree's team, did not orbit. Each time the ball was hit to the infield, each team member was powerfully drawn. The dog pile for the ball was hilarious. Though she is the *Little One*, Aubree came out of that pile with the ball more than once. There was never even a chance to throw the ball to first base. After each melee, the winner came out of the pile holding the ball triumphantly over his or her head. As I watched, I forgot about the Yankees and their struggles.

When she finished, we walked to an adjoining park to practice with the Yankees. Much to my delight, Seth was there with two of his friends. The youngest of the three, Tim Scalia, was on Blake's new team. Seth and Tim must have rushed right home from school and come immediately to the park to play baseball. They were still wearing their school clothes. They were playing a game they had invented themselves. They called it Home Run Derby. As I watched, I remembered the games I played as a boy. There were Two-Man and 500. Home Run Derby was a combination of the two. Once Aubree's practice ended, I started feeling sorry for myself again. I needed help to forget the pressure of building a new team. Even though I'm old, Seth and Tim were kind enough to let me join their game. Again, my troubles disappeared.

As we played, Seth struck up a conversation.

"How's your team doing this year?"

I was hesitant to answer. Tim was there, and I didn't want to discourage him. I felt, however, that I owed Seth an honest answer.

"We're not very good. We've started 0–3. We just don't have much pitching. It's all about pitching."

"I'll bet you'll do better than you think. Maybe you don't remember, but our team started the same way last season."

Without realizing, sometimes boys know exactly what to say. Maybe they do realize. My spirits were lifted. As we finished Home Run Derby, Tim asked a question.

"Are we practicing today?"

"Yes. That's why I'm here. We'll start in about fifteen minutes. You're coming, aren't you?"

"You bet I'm coming!" he said excitedly. "But I forgot some stuff. I think I have enough time to run home for a minute. I'll be right back."

After Tim left, Blake helped me get the gear ready for practice. We pulled out the batting helmets; we hung the bats in the rack; we set out the catcher's gear. We even had time to put the ball bucket near the pitcher's mound. The boys arrived, one by one, all except Tim. He wasn't anywhere to be found. We started taking infield without him.

"I'm here!" he shouted. "I just had to get my glove!"

He stood there proudly, in his Yankee uniform. I hate the New York Yankees. But seeing Tim standing so happily in that uniform brought great joy. It's as close as I'll ever come to being a New York Yankee fan. It's not about the team called the Yankees. It's about the uniform. Even though our team hadn't won a game, Tim didn't care. He felt as if he were part of something special. It didn't have to be a baseball uniform. He could have been wearing choir robes; he could have been wearing a band uniform; he could have been wearing a Scout uniform. It was the uniform that connected him to something bigger than himself. When I played baseball as a boy, I got in trouble for wearing my uniform to practice. We were supposed to keep our uniforms nice for real games. Our coach was furious if we wore our uniform to practice.

I couldn't be mad at Tim.

Since that practice, the Farmington Yankees have won four of five games. We're 4–4 now and climbing in the standings. We knocked the Dodgers out of first place, winning 9–6. We did the same to the first-place Rangers, knocking them out of first place by winning, 5–4. Such scoreboarding doesn't matter. The boys don't care. Their attention is turned to something more important. Just as Blake last season with the Farmington Cubs, all the boys are part of something special, something bigger than themselves this season with the Farmington Yankees. They wear the Farmington Yankee blue. That is enough. In the coming weeks, I hope Tim completely wears out his uniform. He's part of the Farmington Yankees.

Chapter Seventeen—Equilibrium

Seeing Blake in his Cubs' uniform when he stood at the plate on that magical night meant everything to me. It meant far more than the outcome of any of his at-bats. His last turn at bat lasted several pitches, and he finally struck out. Blake was frustrated; I was elated. Blake had batted four times for the Cubs in the FABL Bronco Division championship game.

Tony and Davey, the bottom of the batting order, came to the plate after Blake and also struck out, in succession. Although the inning was over quickly, neither of those other two strikeouts was important either. That Blake, Tony, and Davey all wore the Cubs' uniform was far more significant than any strikeout.

Although the Cubs went down quickly in the top half of the inning, that magical night was far from over. There was still plenty of drama to come. The Rays came to bat in the bottom of the eighth. Seth was facing the top of their order, but he quickly retired the first two batters. Then, like a volcano pushing outward at the earth's crust, events became heated. The Rays' number three hitter singled and then advanced to third by stealing the bases. The Rays' cleanup hitter then stepped to the plate. He ran the count to two balls and two strikes. Seth readied to make his next pitch. He started the delivery and then held up; he didn't let go of the ball. The move was clearly a balk. Ted came screaming from the dugout again. He strutted to the umpire as if he were a French emperor. I was beginning to think there was no need for umpires. Wasn't it up to the boys to determine the winner?

In *Les Misérables*, Victor Hugo spoke to Napoleon and condensed domain:

> The excessive weight of this man in human destiny disturbed the equilibrium. This individual counted, of himself alone, more than the universe besides. These plethoras of all human vitality concentrated in a single head, the world mounting to the brain of one man, would be fatal to civilization if they should endure. The moment had come for incorruptible supreme equity to look to it. Probably the principles and elements upon which regular gravitations in the moral order as well as in the material depend, began to murmur.... When the earth is suffering from a surcharge, there are mysterious moanings from the deep which the heavens hear.[8]

Although this was only a baseball game, an explanation of the world was in order. Ted did not count more than the universe besides; this was Blake's universe. Though all men truly have their agency, we are fools when we believe we can sway the equilibrium of universal events. Even if events unfold as we hope, if we believe those results were within our control, we lack understanding.

"That was a balk!" Ted yelled. "You have to make that call. The pitcher balked!"

Seth had indeed balked, but there were moanings from the deep. There was no way the Cubs were going to lose on a cheap called balk. This time an attempt to sway the equilibrium would not be allowed. The league rules were clear, and they, if not the laws of the universe, were on my side. The Bronco Division was

---

8   Victor Hugo, *Les Misérables*, trans. Charles E. Wilbour (New York: Random House, 1992), Cosette, Book I, page 288.

instructional. No balks had been called all season. The umpires had been told in the event of a balk the pitcher was to receive warning and was instructed as to his error, and play continued. I came out of the dugout to argue a call for the first time that evening. I held nothing back. I didn't think Amanda would disapprove. The argument wasn't about me. It was about the broader view. I didn't pretend to address the umpire; I spoke directly to Ted.

"Coach, this is an instructional league. That call hasn't been made all season. Tell the pitcher what he did wrong, and let's play."

"But this is the championship game!" Ted blared. "The call needs to be made right now! Send the runner home from third, and the game is over!"

"Coach, the call shouldn't be made. The rules are clear; the pitcher gets a warning before a balk is called. Give my pitcher the warning, and let's play! And while you're at it, you need to pull your head out of your ass!"

Okay. Maybe I went too far. Amanda probably wouldn't have approved of *everything*. The crowd groaned. Understand, this was Farmington, *Utah*. In most places the comment would have been ignored; it wouldn't be in Farmington. I had uttered the unforgivable, and it appeared the consequences were coming.

The umpire turned abruptly. "Hey, we're not going to have any of that kind of talk here!"

I knew I was on the edge, so I quickly turned, turned even before the umpire could make eye contact, and moved toward the dugout. I was laughing to myself as I approached the team.

Wow! Where did that come from? I wondered as I walked, head bowed, to the dugout. *I shouldn't have said it, but it was pretty funny. I hope none of the boys heard.*

I caught Bob Henderson's eye as I neared home plate.

"You didn't hear that, did you?"

"What? The part about the guy's head being stuck in an unnatural part of his anatomy? Yeah, I heard it. But it's okay. You only said what everyone else was thinking."

Amanda then came from nowhere.

"Hi, Dad! What's up?" Amanda was back. "Can I get a Diet Coke with my hot dog?"

I handed her another dollar while we waited for the outcome. The umpires deliberated and then came to their decision. No balk was called; Seth was given a warning, and play continued. I was even allowed to remain at the game. Ted stormed back to his dugout. I thought I saw him turn, stand stiffly, and stuff his hand into his shirt. The best two dollars I ever spent. With the score tied and two outs, the Rays' cleanup hitter waited to finish his at-bat. The boy hit the ball hard every time he had been to the plate.

"What's the count, Bob?"

Bob had faithfully kept the scorebook the entire evening. When I needed him most, he was ready.

"It's 2–2. You ought to put him on base."

It made sense. I told Seth to throw two pitchouts to put the batter on base. The number five hitter then came to the plate. Bob explained this batter had also hit the ball hard every time he had been at bat. The number six hitter had struck out two of three times. We were playing the percentages. We determined to walk the number five hitter also, to load up the bases.

So it all came down to one hitter. One last at-bat. The drum beat for Seth. For the first time, Seth had come to understand rhythm. He had pitched brilliantly. The moment was similar to Justin's service to Blakey. The lines of Seth's potential and performance crossed. He comprehended the flow of baseball's universe. The at-bat progressed, and the count was full. Now it was down to one pitch.

Seth let the pitch go, and the batter made contact. From the center of his universe, a boy I didn't know reached out and grabbed a host of dreams. He hit a routine grounder to short. Sky was there to make the play, but he bobbled the ball. He just couldn't get it out of his glove. All that was needed was a timely throw to first base for the out, but it wasn't to be. The runner from third base scored, and the game was over. It was a miracle in the Rays' universe and a miracle in my universe. It was the miracle of Blake.

Chapter Eighteen—Authentic

There was no reason to be angry at Sky. He played a terrific game. He had made several plays that kept the Cubs in the contest. There wasn't any need to be upset by the loss. Although no one enjoys losing, for the first time as either a coach or a player, I didn't care. The Cubs did everything they knew to win. The better team had not won because there was no better team. Only one bounce of the ball determined the outcome.

What a game it was. A game of flow; a game of rhythm.

In spite of the loss, the entire night seemed surreal. I didn't know whether the Cubs realized the finished game's import. The team with the mockingbirds had made it all the way to the championship. The team with mockingbirds had missed first place by only one bounce of the ball. Neither had the Rays won by petty argument, their hero dragged from the center of his world by misdirected competition.

And in Blake's world, the box score for the game read that Blakey had been to bat four times and struck out every one. The causal reader of that box would probably miss the most important statistic. Blake William Curtis had been to the plate four times in a championship game; no, Blake Curtis had been to the plate four times in *the* championship game, the championship game played at the center of the universe.

The Rays' celebration was emotional. Exultant father met champion son with unbridled joy, rejoicing together in the game-winning hit. The father lifted his son, that unknown hero from across the universe, into the air, and they danced in rhythm. That such joy was displayed after a victory over the Cubs was testament to how far the mockingbirds had come. I accepted the compliment with a smile. Then I looked for Sky. I wanted to make sure he knew he had no reason to hang his head. I found him standing with his posse at the plate, immortalizing *the catch*. Sky was in his element. He was happy. I congratulated Ted. Wins that don't come easily are far more satisfying than runaway victories or those grabbed on inaccurate technicalities. He reveled in the moment with his team and in a victory won by a hero, not by an imperial edict.

The Cubs then gathered in a circle, one more time. They put their hands on mine in the center and shouted for the Rays. It could easily have been the Rays congratulating the Cubs, and the team knew, in its twelve-year-old way, that the moment should be untainted. Although disappointed, the boys understood sportsmanship.

Seth took the loss hard. I reassured him. He laughed as I turned his cap sideways. Seth had grown light-years since the beginning of the season. He played in perfect rhythm. Collin stood proudly with his mother and father. His dad put his arm around Collin and congratulated him. Collin was more than a ballplayer, and his understanding of love was on Blake's level. Davey's mom pulled Blake away to snap a picture with her son and Blake at home plate. Then, finally, perception's haze lifted. Parents of both teams surrounded Blake. They shook his hand; they put their arms around him; they held him close. Blake's teammates were no longer alone. Others had gained greater understanding of the rhythm of the universe.

It was all so good; it was almost too much. I was overcome. I went alone to the dugout for my usual postgame routine, in search of solitude. I gathered the team's equipment for the last time. The catcher's glove, the shin guards, the chest protector, the four batting helmets. I was silent as I contemplated the evening's events.

This was Blake's universe, but they were *all my Cubs*. I struck the ball straight down the middle of the fairway.

All in flow; all in rhythm.

The league officials put together the awards ceremony for the teams. I summoned all my Cubs to the first baseline so that each player could receive his trophy. Blake had retired to the dugout and would not come out. He was angry about the loss. I beckoned, but he would not move. The chants began. "Blake! Blake! Blake!" The beat could be heard throughout Farmington, throughout the center of the universe. Then he came, came out from the shadows, to accept his trophy. All my Cubs, and the Rays as well, had joined together to acknowledge him. All their parents, all their friends, all their worlds gathered as one, if for only a moment, to support my son.

In his poem "The Three Voices," Robert Service wrote:

> But the stars throng out in their glory,
>   And they sing of the God in man;
> They sing of the Mighty Master,
>   Of the loom his fingers span,
> Where a star or a soul is part of the whole,
>   And weft in the wondrous plan.[9]

If only for a moment, it was as if the cloud cover over Farmington had lifted. The stars shined brightly. Blake belonged. He was woven into the song, the beat, and the rhythm of nested worlds.

---

9   Robert Service, "The Three Voices," *Collected Poems of Robert Service* (New York: G.P. Putnam's Sons, 1940), 8.

Blake answered with his greatest gift. He loved. He loved all his fellow baseball players, and all of his teammates, back. He loved all the parents, and he loved all the friends. Blake stood happily, holding his trophy in his hands, the true champion he is, as he loved them. There is no greater gift.

Ryan West spotted me as I finished stowing the gear. "Here, Coach," he quietly said. "I brought you a baseball for Blake. We're glad to have him in the league."

I took the ball in my hand and thanked Ryan. Then I gathered my team one more time.

"Gentlemen, the league president gave me a game ball for Blakey. Would all of you take a minute to sign it for him?"

———

Years before, my son Tyler had played on a traveling baseball team. On a cold spring morning, his team faced a club from Alpine, Utah. Dale Murphy, formerly of the Atlanta Braves and the MVP in the National League for both the 1982 and 1983 seasons, coached the Alpine team. He was my childhood hero. When I saw him, I was a giddy schoolboy all over again. I did everything I could to avoid him. I thought I was too old to still feel that way. Another man in the stands also recognized him. That man went home and returned with his Ken Burns *Baseball* book. He asked Murphy to sign it. He said it was for his son.

I laughed out loud. I couldn't resist. I spoke to Murphy.

"Do you really think you're signing for his son?"

Murphy answered with a smile. "I'm sure I'm not. I'm too old for anyone that age to know me now."

The man didn't fool Murphy. Did I fool my Cubs?

———

As the ceremony wound down, we gathered one more time for a few pictures at home plate. Parents from both teams approached and openly reveled in the conclusion of a great season. Chris Jacobson was the first to join me.

"Coach," he said, carefully considering the title, "I want to thank you for a great year. It was the best season Tony has ever had."

Chris paused; we shook hands and looked eye to eye. No other words were spoken. I understood the meaning of the brief conversation, as conveyed from one father of a boy with disability to another.

A Rays' parent followed. Together we also took the opportunity to enjoy the moment. Although I never knew his name, I had discussed baseball with the man for years. We were talking and laughing as Blake quietly drew near.

When I talk to someone Blake doesn't know, he feels the need to introduce us. It doesn't matter if I already know with whom I'm chatting. If Blake doesn't know them, formal introductions are in order. I stopped and waited. Blake stood, turned both palms up, and motioned toward me with both hands.

"Um, excuse me, sir. This my dad. He my coach."

The title was bestowed. When Blake was through, the man looked up and paid the highest compliment he had to offer.

"Coach, I would have my son play on your team anytime."

There was neither a better team nor a better group of parents on that magical night. In time's continuum, if only for a brief moment, one and all knew they stood in the center of Blake's world. Blake was aware.

Everyone was in tune. Harmonious flow; harmonious rhythm.

Chapter Nineteen—My World

I returned from this reverie as I approached the pizzeria. I brushed the tears from my face one more time, regained composure, and entered to settle with Sharon.

"How did it go?" she asked.

I shuffled the empty pizza bags on the shelf; I jingled my keys in my pants pocket; I adjusted my uniform cap; finally, I pulled the crumpled twenty-dollar bill from my other pocket and smoothed it.

"It was okay. Can we total my receipts now so I can go home?"

Sharon totaled the evening's deliveries quickly, and I was on my way. I didn't know if Sharon noticed my red eyes and tear-stained face. I didn't care. It had been a difficult night, and I felt a great need to stand at the center of the universe.

A baseball is hidden away in a remote corner of my closet. It has not been hit or thrown, and it has never seen the dirt of an infield or the grass of an outfield. It is not dusty. I pull it out of the closet from time to time, pull it out when I feel the need to stand at the center of the universe.

And on that night I took the ball into my hands and looked at the signatures. Then I held it close to my face. It reeked the infield's sweet perfume. I heard them all. I saw them all. Seth, throwing bullet pitches, in perfect rhythm; Collin, executing the perfect squeeze bunt, scoring Chase; Pete, the look of joy in his eyes, hitting a triple to score two more; Buck, *the fastest of them all*, motoring around the bases; Tony, focused and attentive, stealing second; Justin, stealing home, without hesitation; Sky, talking smack to anyone willing to listen, hitting a triple in the championship game; Johnny, smiling broadly, proud of his contribution; Davey, pitching nothing but strikes, smiling after every pitch; Jared, the human vacuum cleaner, catching everything hit to second base; Chase, teaching Blake to catch, without ever making a throw.

But, to my remembering, I remembered Blake.

I remembered Blake William Curtis, #9, as he stood at bat in a real baseball game, a real championship baseball game, the game at the center of the universe. I remembered seeing the light in Blake's eyes as he hit the ball over the fence, not caring it was foul and out of play. I remembered seeing the smile rifle across his face as he dropped his bat and raced toward first base. I remembered seeing his ungainly gait, the gait in perfect flow, the gait in perfect rhythm, as he headed to his spot in right field. I remembered hearing the music, "Blake, Blake, Blake," from all my Cubs, all my mockingbirds, singing, in perfect pitch.

All in flow; all in rhythm.

Epilogue

It's the close of another season.

Interesting.

When the season began, I met Sam Beck. Sam is the boy from across the universe; he is the boy that knocked in the game-winning RBI for the championship. He really is a great boy. He's on our team this year. As I was putting this year's team together, I had no idea who he was. Not until I made *the phone call.* After I introduced Blakey and me, I talked a little longer with Sam's mom, and we figured it out. She happily told me about the previous season, about how Sam had pushed the game-winning run across the plate for first place. I immediately remembered Sam. It took Mrs. Beck a little longer to remember us, but eventually she put the pieces together. I am, after all, the only coach in the league who has a son with Down syndrome playing. That and she was also nearby during the final moments of the game when I explained to Sam's coach his unusual anatomical position. Mrs. Beck offered some insight into Sam. Sam had explained his feelings to her about his hit. For an eleven-year-old, he was perceptive. I don't remember exactly how she retold what he said, but I've captured its essence.

"Everyone has a moment in their life where they are the center of the universe, a moment when all eyes are focused on them and they are the shining star. That was my moment."

It is a moment when a boy can reach out and grab a host of dreams.

The other day I met another of the parents who was involved with the Rays. He came into the pizza joint to order a pie. We laughed as we reminisced about that magical night. He talked about Sam and the final at-bat.

"You did exactly what you should have when you told your pitcher to walk the two batters before Sam. Pitching to him was the thing to do. We were scared to death. We thought he would strike out for sure. We didn't think there was any way he would make contact with the ball."

Years ago, I was at my father's bedside when he passed. The experience was difficult and sad, but it was also amazing. For the first time, I saw my father through different eyes. Rather than as my father, I saw him as a man like myself, a man searching for his own understanding as to the operation of the universe. There are events in our lives that help us see with clarity. Even baseball games can open our minds to different possibilities. Billy Chapel was right to want to involve God in a baseball game. However, rather than praying for wins, a man ought to pray for understanding. A man ought to pray to see things as they are.

Sam's parents are divorced. A divorce is never easy for anyone. Sam is a far better boy than he is a baseball player. That game-winning hit was incredibly important to him. He needed that hit far more than my team needed to win the championship. His father hasn't made it any easier. During a game this season, Sam's father was upset with me. We were losing, and he was frustrated. First, he took his anger out on the boys of our team. He sat behind our catcher and told him he was a bad player. When that didn't work, when I didn't respond, he stood behind our team's parents with mutiny in mind. He tried to stir them to the same level of anger he felt. After that didn't work, he confronted me directly.

"I don't like what you're doing. I don't like how you're coaching. I think you should play someone else."

I'm not approachable during a game. I'm compartmental; I focus on the task at hand. I'm especially not approachable during a baseball game if someone has been unfairly criticizing a twelve-year-old or if someone has been trying to stir a parent mutiny. I answered.

"You're not helping. You need to sit down and shut up. If you want to coach, sign up for your own team next season."

I was angry. I've coached for many years, and most parents have left me alone. I can count on one hand the number of times I've had a parent try to interfere like Sam's father did that night. It hasn't happened very often, but it does happen. Blake was there to help me remember. He reminded me why I'm willing to listen to an occasional angry parent.

Blake came to the plate in *full ritual mode* right after the confrontation with Sam's dad. The boys on the opposing team were unaware. They hadn't paid attention to the shouting match, and they weren't concerned when they saw Blake come to bat. The shortstop drifted in from the base path dirt to the infield grass and then moved toward second base. The third baseman joined him. They stood together talking as Blake got ready for the pitch. The pitcher fired the ball. Blake ripped a screaming liner down the third baseline, right where the third baseman should have been standing. He hit the ball so hard that it reached the outfield fence. Although the hit was a clean double, Blake's gait took him only to first base. I smiled. I remembered. Blake's hit made it all worthwhile.

I haven't seen Sam's dad since our confrontation. It's been quite a bit easier to focus on Sam; it's been easier to help Sam understand *The Rhythm of the Game*. It would be easy to believe that it's a coincidence Sam is on my team this year; it would be easy to rationalize such a universe after being on the losing end of that final score in the previous season's championship game. I don't think so. The wonder of our existence lies in putting all those *coincidences* together and making sense of them. And although Sam's comments about his game-winning hit are insightful, they don't tell the entire story. The universal moment Sam referred to is not limited to just one. Sam will live many more wonderful moments as he sees his dreams fulfilled.

Blake is having another great season. The boys on the team, their parents, and the entire league have been terrific. I was playing catch with Blake the other day before a game. He smiled and spoke.

"Dad, I pitch to you? Like Ty?"

"Sure, Blake, you can pitch to me."

I crouched down into the catcher position. Rather than facing me directly, Blake turned to where third base would have been. Both his arms hung loosely to his sides. He gripped the ball in his right hand; he wore his glove on his left. He brought both arms up over his head simultaneously and then down again to his chest, putting the ball in his glove. He glanced over his left shoulder, seeing an imaginary runner on first base. Then he lifted his left leg toward me and threw the ball. The pitch wasn't perfect, but the windup was. I'd never shown him the windup. I suppose he learned by watching the boys, just as he learned to catch by watching Chase Everett. The genesis of an idea came to me. We worked together on the windup. We went to the ballpark early, and Blake learned to throw off the mound. When I thought he was ready, the idea became a plan. We were playing the Rangers. I found their coach.

"Coach, Blake wants to pitch. Would it be all right if we tried? Toward the end of the game, I'll choose an inning when your team is at bat. After we get the third out, I'll wave to you. I'll keep my team in their positions on the field. You pick whomever you want

- 148 -

to bat. Send him to the plate. I don't care what he does. He can crush the ball if he wants. Just let Blake pitch to him."

The Rangers' coach was great.

"I'd love to see Blake pitch. You let me know when."

I talked to the umpires so they would know what we were doing. I had my camera phone with me. I went to Brittany Child. She and Sam's mom have alternated keeping the scorebook this season. I was hoping she would take a few pictures. When I tried to talk to her, the words wouldn't come. I get really emotional over silly things now. Brit panicked.

"Jeff, are you okay? Is something wrong?"

When I got control, I explained the plan.

"Blake is going to pitch to a batter. It's all been worked out with the Rangers' coach. Can you take a few pictures for me?"

Brit was terrific.

"I have my camera here with me. In fact, I think I even brought my video camera."

I thanked her and left as quickly as I could. The game was about to start. The game moved along, and in the bottom of the fifth inning, Steve Child, Brit's son, retired the side. I waved to the other coach. The Yankees were already coming off the field. I motioned them to stay. The team was confused. Tim Scalia questioned.

"Coach, it was the third out. We're up to bat."

I hadn't told the boys about the plan. I didn't even tell Blake. I especially didn't tell Blake.

"Just stay on the field a little longer. We're going to do something different." Then I turned to Blake. He was standing in his spot in right field. I waved my arm as I called. "Blake, come here."

Blake looked every direction except toward me. He was teasing. It's his way. I called to him again.

"Blake, come here!"

He looked down at the grass, avoiding eye contact. In his mind, if he doesn't acknowledge me, I don't exist. Then he is free to do as he pleases. I had to ramp up the negotiation.

"Blake, do you want to pitch?"

This was unexpected. He was surprised. He looked over both shoulders, and then he looked to me. As he did so, he lifted his right arm in a big, sweeping motion and pointed to himself.

"Me?"

"Yes, you. Do you want to pitch? Like Ty?"

"Yeah!"

"Well, come on then!"

He charged toward the mound. As he stood with his foot on the rubber, I lost control again. The tears freely flowed. I couldn't speak. Blake never makes it easy for me. He innocently looked to me.

"Dad, what's wrong?"

I forced myself to choke out, "Throw some strikes," as I handed him the ball. I left as quickly as I could. I knelt in front of the dugout. Beth and Greg Anderson, the assistant coach, had the picture-taking well in hand. I just wanted to watch.

Blake started his windup. He let go of the ball. The pitch had little velocity, but it was a perfect strike. The Rangers player let it go by. The umpire then made the call.

"Strike one!"

Carlton Beach, the Yankee catcher, then threw the ball back to Blake. Blake stabbed it with his glove. Then he began again. His second pitch was identical to the first. It was right over the plate.

"Strike two!"

Carlton threw the ball back to Blake again, and Blake missed the throw. After he tracked down the ball, he readied for his next pitch. He wound up and let the ball go. The pitch was high and outside. The batter swung and missed.

"Strike three, you're out!"

Both teams surrounded Blake and congratulated him. It was over far too quickly.

I've often questioned my own motives as Blake plays baseball. Have I done it for him, or do I do it for myself? Have I completely dealt with his disability? Am I trying to make him something he's not? I'm not deaf to the talk. Most have been really great, but I know there are those who think it's all a big show. In the movie *The Blind Side*, the lead, Leigh Ann Tuohy, asks her husband, "Am I a good person?"[10]

I loved the movie, but I hated that line. It seems to me if you have to ask a question like that, you already know the answer, and it isn't what you're hoping for. But I'm not so hard on Mrs. Tuohy now. I've lived that dilemma myself.

I'm so lucky to be near Blake. He's answered my questions. Kristi had some commitments that forced her to be late to the game in which Blake pitched. We drove in separate cars. Blake was with her on the way home. She listened while he had a conversation with himself. He even answered back; he was in his own world. In his discussion, he was actually talking to me. I was the other speaker, but Blake did all the talking.

---

10 "Don't You Dare Lie," *The Blind Side*, directed by John Lee Hancock (Burbank, CA: Warner Brothers, 2009), DVD.

"Blake, come here."

"Me?"

"Yes, you. You want to pitch?"

"Yes, I pitch."

"Okay. Here's the ball."

"Okay." Then he smiled. I know I told you I wasn't there. I wasn't. Yet I know that he smiled broadly. I know Blake. He smiled with his eyes.

"Strike one! Strike two! Strike three, you out!"

I do it for Blake, but he sure makes it feels like it's for me.

All in flow; all in rhythm.

Author's Note

The events detailed in *The Rhythm of the Game* unfolded pretty much as they are written. There are a few differences where I used some license. I wanted to explain them for my own historical record. I want my children to know and to remember the events as they happened.

I wasn't driving Tyler's jeep when I delivered that first pizza. It cost too much for gas. I was driving my own car. I put myself in the jeep to add drama. And I didn't take the pizza job to pay for Tyler's college. I did it to support him on his Mormon mission. I wrote it was for college because more people understand college than understand missions.

Ted Thompson was not the coach arguing for the balk to be called at the end of the championship game. It was one of his assistants. Ted stood nearby, but he didn't argue the call. He did, as I recall, argue every other call that I wrote about in the book.

And finally, for the record, I didn't actually tell Ted's assistant to pull his head out of his ass. I told him to pull his head out of his *rear end*. Even that euphemism was too much for Farmington's residents. They reacted just as it was written. It still makes me laugh when I remember the unison, audible "ooohhh" that they sang out after I said what I said.

They said it in rhythm; they said it in flow.

With Ann Reich looking on, Blake looks for his spot in the batting order.

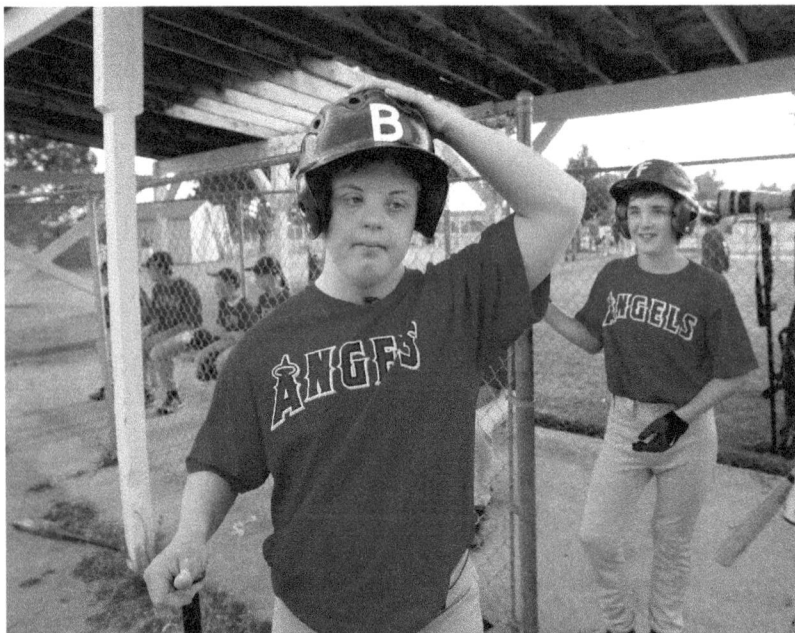

Under Jaxon Cummings' watchful eye, Blake gets ready to bat.

Blake waves to his teammates. In the background, from left to right,
Caden Cornford, Max Johnson, and Jacob Miller.

Blake goes to work at the plate, telling the umpire "I watching you!"

Babe Ruth style, Blake calls his shot. He stole the pose from the "Whammer," his favorite character in "The Natural."

. . . And makes contact.

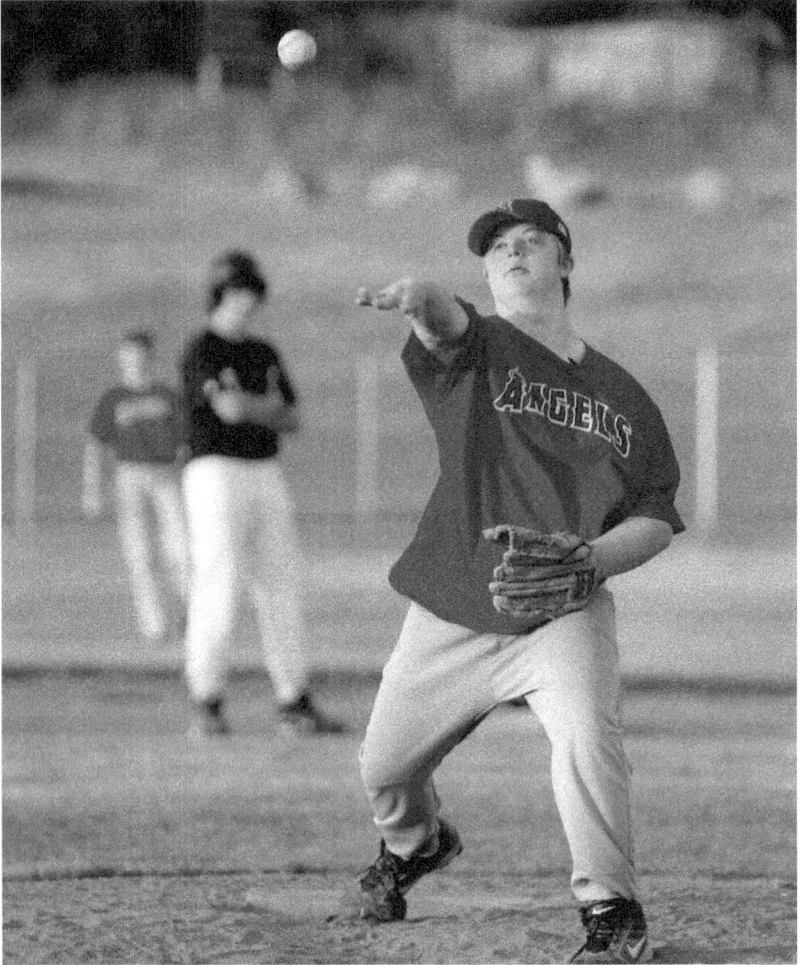

Blake cuts loose with his version of a curve ball, just like his
big brother, Ty.

Jaxon Cummings congratulates Blake as they walk together to the dugout.

After pitching to the game's last batter, Blake is surrounded by his teammates, Caden Cornford, Hayden Jung, and Devin Carlile. Ann Reich (left) and Jacob Miller are in the background.

Blake's dad, Jeff, congratulates Blake for making it all the way to third base.

www.ingramcontent.com/pod-product-compliance
Lightning Source LLC
Chambersburg PA
CBHW020536100426
42813CB00038B/3468/J

* 9 7 8 0 9 8 8 4 2 7 6 6 2 *